P9-BYU-013

STOP!

This is the back of the book. You wouldn't want to spoil a great ending!

This book is printed "manga-style," in the authentic Japanese right-to-left format. Since none of the artwork has been flipped or altered, readers get to experience the story just as the creator intended. You've been asking for it, so TOKYOPOP® delivered: authentic, hot-off-the-press, and far more fun!

DIRECTIONS

If this is your first time reading manga-style, here's a quick guide to help you understand how it works.

It's easy... just start in the top right panel and follow the numbers. Have fun, and look for more 100% authentic manga from TOKYOPOP®!

品質第一公式商品
100%
AUTHENTIC
MANGA

ALSO AVAILABLE FROM TOKYOPOP®

MANGA

.HACK//LEGEND OF THE TWILIGHT
@LARGE
ABENOBASHI: MAGICAL SHOPPING ARCADE
A.I. LOVE YOU
AI YORI AOSHI
ALICHINO
ANGELIC LAYER
ARM OF KANNON
BABY BIRTH
BATTLE ROYALE
BATTLE VIXENS
BOYS BE...
BRAIN POWERED
BRIGADOON
B'TX
CANDIDATE FOR GODDESS, THE
CARDCAPTOR SAKURA
CARDCAPTOR SAKURA - MASTER OF THE CLOW
CHOBITS
CHRONICLES OF THE CURSED SWORD
CLAMP SCHOOL DETECTIVES
CLOVER
COMIC PARTY
CONFIDENTIAL CONFESSIONS
CORRECTOR YUI
COWBOY BEBOP
COWBOY BEBOP: SHOOTING STAR
CRAZY LOVE STORY
CRESCENT MOON
CROSS
CULDCEPT
CYBORG 009
D•N•ANGEL
DEARS
DEMON DIARY
DEMON ORORON, THE
DEUS VITAE
DIGIMON
DIGIMON TAMERS
DIGIMON ZERO TWO
DOLL
DRAGON HUNTER
DRAGON KNIGHTS
DRAGON VOICE
DREAM SAGA
DUKLYON: CLAMP SCHOOL DEFENDERS
EERIE QUEERIE!
ERICA SAKURAZAWA: COLLECTED WORKS
ET CETERA
ETERNITY
EVIL'S RETURN
FAERIES' LANDING
FAKE
FLCL
FLOWER OF THE DEEP SLEEP, THE
FORBIDDEN DANCE
FRUITS BASKET
G GUNDAM
GATEKEEPERS
GETBACKERS
GIRL GOT GAME
GRAVITATION
GTO
GUNDAM SEED ASTRAY
GUNDAM WING
GUNDAM WING: BATTLEFIELD OF PACIFISTS
GUNDAM WING: ENDLESS WALTZ
GUNDAM WING: THE LAST OUTPOST (G-UNIT)
HANDS OFF!
HAPPY MANIA
HARLEM BEAT
HYPER RUNE
I.N.V.U.
IMMORTAL RAIN
INITIAL D
INSTANT TEEN: JUST ADD NUTS
ISLAND
JING: KING OF BANDITS
JING: KING OF BANDITS - TWILIGHT TALES
JULINE
KARE KANO
KILL ME, KISS ME
KINDAICHI CASE FILES, THE
KING OF HELL
KODOCHA: SANA'S STAGE
LAMENT OF THE LAMB
LEGAL DRUG
LEGEND OF CHUN HYANG, THE
LES BIJOUX
LOVE HINA
LOVE OR MONEY
LUPIN III
LUPIN III: WORLD'S MOST WANTED
MAGIC KNIGHT RAYEARTH I
MAGIC KNIGHT RAYEARTH II
MAHOROMATIC: AUTOMATIC MAIDEN
MAN OF MANY FACES
MARMALADE BOY
MARS
MARS: HORSE WITH NO NAME
MINK
MIRACLE GIRLS
MIYUKI-CHAN IN WONDERLAND
MODEL
MOURYOU KIDEN: LEGEND OF THE NYMPHS
NECK AND NECK
ONE
ONE I LOVE, THE
PARADISE KISS
PARASYTE
PASSION FRUIT
PEACH GIRL
PEACH GIRL: CHANGE OF HEART
PET SHOP OF HORRORS
PITA-TEN
PLANET LADDER

08.20.04T

Fruits Basket™

Volume 6

By
Natsuki Takaya

TOKYOPOP®

HAMBURG // LONDON // LOS ANGELES // TOKYO

Fruits Basket™

Table of Contents

Chapter 31 9
Chapter 32 40
Chapter 33 73
Chapter 34 103
Chapter 35 165
Year of the Rabbit 198
Fans Basket 199

STORY SO FAR...

Hello, I'm Tohru Honda, and I have come to know a terrible secret. After the death of my mother, I was living by myself in a tent when the Sohma family took me in. I soon learned that the Sohma family lives with a curse! Each family member is possessed by the vengeful spirit of an animal from the Chinese Zodiac. Whenever one of them becomes weak or is hugged by a member of the opposite sex, they change into their Zodiac animal!

Tohru Honda

The ever-optimistic hero of our story. An orphan, she now lives in Shigure's house, along with Yuki and Kyo, and is the only person outside of the family who knows the Sohma family's curse.

Yuki Sohma, the Rat

Soft-spoken. Self-esteem issues.
At school he's called "Prince Yuki."

Kyo Sohma, the Cat

The Cat who was left out of the Zodiac.
Hates Yuki, leeks and Miso. But mostly Yuki.

Mabudachi Trio

Shigure Sohma, the Dog

Enigmatic, mischievous and a little perverted. A popular novelist.

Hatori Sohma, the Dragon

Family doctor to the Sohmas. Only thing he can't cure is his broken heart.

Ayame Sohma, the Snake

Yuki's older brother. A proud and playful drama queen…er, king. Runs a costume shop.

Fruits Basket Characters

Kagura Sohma, the Boar

Bashful, yet headstrong. Determined to marry Kyo, even if it kills him.

Momiji Sohma, the Rabbit

Half-German. He's older than he looks. Mother rejected him because of the Sohma curse.

Hatsuharu Sohma, the Ox

The nicest of guys, except when he goes "Black." Then you'd better watch out.

Akito Sohma

The head of the Sohma clan. A dark figure of many secrets. Treated with fear and reverence.

Tohru's Best Friends

Saki Hanajima

"Hana-chan." Can sense people's "waves." Goth demeanor scares her classmates.

Arisa Uotani

"Uo-chan." A tough-talking "Yankee" who looks out for her friends.

Kisa Sohma, the Tiger

Kisa became shy and self-conscious due to constant teasing by her classmates. Yuki, who has similar insecurities, feels particularly close to Kisa.

Fruits Basket™

Chapter 31

ULTRA-SPECIAL BLAH BLAH BLAH 1

I've been going through some hard times lately.
And on top of that, I had a fever of over 105°.
It's like Punch, Punch, Kick!
By the way, I tend to get sick on rainy days.

THE WEATHER REPORT SAID IT WOULD LET UP A LITTLE THIS AFTERNOON.
IF IT DOES STOP, THAT WOULD BE VERY HELPFUL.
BUT WHAT WOULD BE EVEN **MORE** HELPFUL IS IF IT TURNED OUT TO BE A CLEAR, SUNNY SUMMER!

DO YOU LIKE SUMMER, YUKI-KUN?
HOW LIKE HONDA-SAN...
MM... I GUESS YOU COULD SAY IT'S NOT MY **FAVORITE** SEASON...

SUMMER, HUH...
YOU REALLY LIKE SUMMER, HONDA-SAN?
Yes!
I CAN WORK A LOT DURING SUMMER BREAK.

YOU LIKE SUMMER, DON'T YOU, KYO-KUN?!
REALLY...?
AH!

*awkward silence
む〜〜ん
.....
I DON'T KNOW. I DON'T REALLY CARE ONE WAY OR THE OTHER.
UM...
ER... WELL...
HONDA-SAN...? HONDA-SAN?
Kyo-kun, are you going to bed already?
NO!
?
I see...
SO THAT'S WHY HE'S BEEN IN SUCH A BAD MOOD LATELY.
SO IT WOULD SEEM.
REALLY, HE'S SO IRRESPONSIBLE.
GRRR!
IT'S NOTHING TO WORRY ABOUT.
HE ALWAYS GETS THIS WAY ON RAINY DAYS.
Haru was saying something about it.
OH?

out of energy
ぐたぁ
IN THE... MORNING...
IT'S--
...WAKE UP...
--BETTER THAN YOU, DAMMIT! YOU CAN'T EVEN...
IF YOU'RE HAVING A HARD TIME HOLDING YOUR UMBRELLA...
...PLEASE, SHARE MINE.
worry worry
OH NO! HE'S REALLY NOT LOOKING WELL. IS HE SICK?
DAMMIT! THIS SUCKS!
AH! OH YEAH!
KYO-KUN! IF YOU'RE NOT FEELING WELL, YOU SHOULDN'T PUSH YOURSELF.

*blush
...
L-
LOOK, YOU...!
?
YES?
DON'T "YES?" ME!! WHY...
WHY WOULD I... STAND UNDER A-- A GIRL'S UMBRELLA THAT A GIRL IS HOLDING?!
EH ?!
AH! I-I'M SORRY! THAT IS... UM... WELL...
I KNOW YOU DON'T REALLY LIKE TO, BUT MAYBE IF YOU TURNED INTO A CAT--
--I KNOW IT'S KIND OF FORWARD OF ME-- BUT MAYBE I COULD HUG YOU AND CARRY YOU HO--
THAT'S EVEN WORSE, YOU MORON !!!

Y-YES! I'M SORRY...
UGH... Y...! YOU DON'T HAVE TO APOLOGIZE!
B-BUT...
HONDA-SAN... LET'S GO.
YOU'RE MAKIN' ME EVEN MORE TIRED!!
YOU WORRY TOO MUCH ABOUT EVERYTHING!!
Aaaugh!
Haah?
HELL NO! IT'S JUST HOW I AM... LIKE A CONDITION.
A-condition?!
UM...
DO YOU THINK YOU HAVE SOME KIND OF ILLNESS?

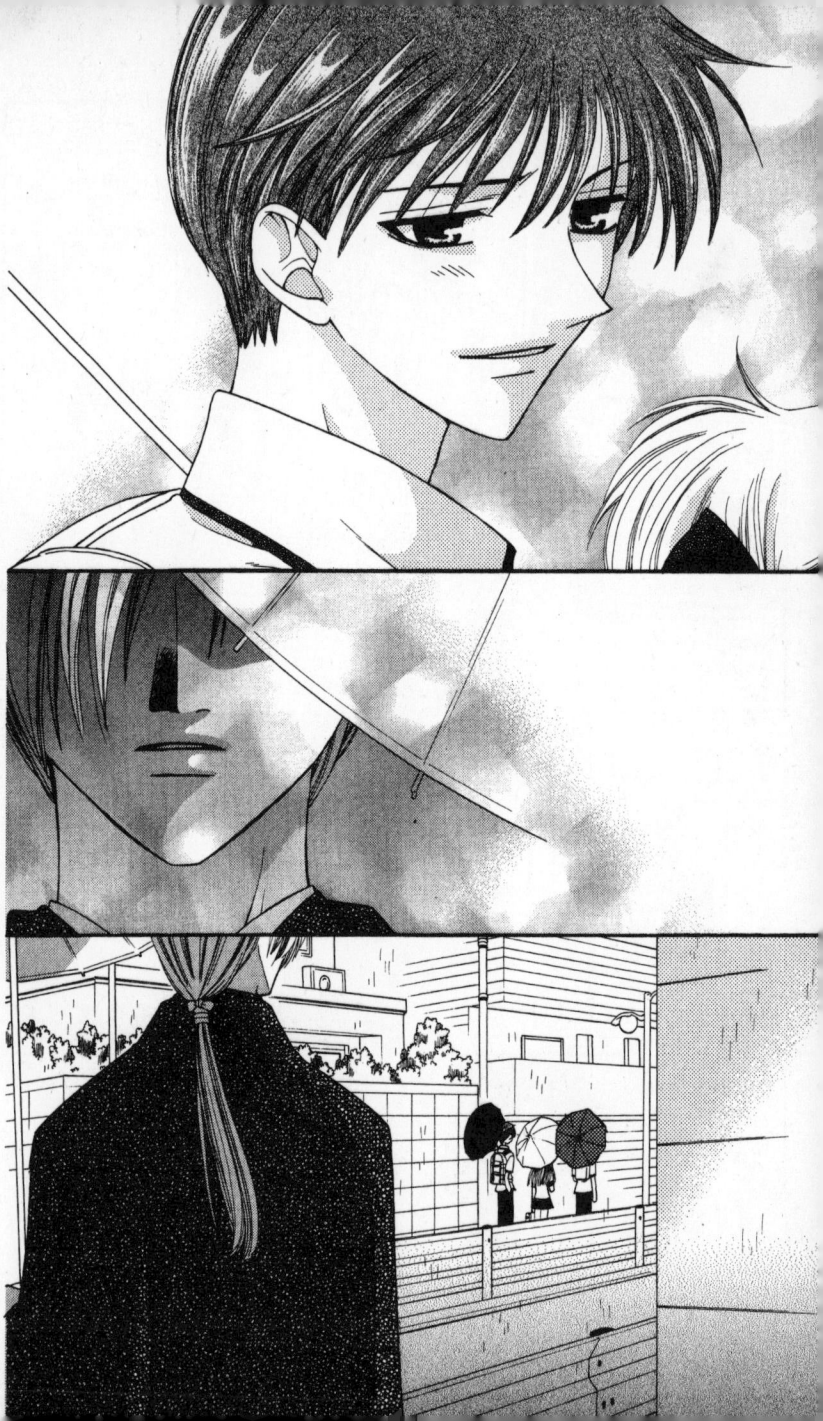

Fruits Basket 6 Part 1:

Hajimemashite and hello! I'm Takaya. Furuba has made it to the sixth volume. That means it's been almost two years since I started drawing it. Woooow... (Gazing into the distance.) So the Volume 6 cover features Momiji. You know, **Momitchi!** He looks very young, but inside, he's the most mature of his generation of Sohmas. Right? "He had to be mature to deal with his youthful appearance and parental situation, right?" Well, yeah. It's kinda sad that way. But I also made him that way because it's cute! Recently, my hand hasn't been doing very well, so my handwriting is harder to read than usual, so gomen nasai. (I'm sorry!) Please enjoy Volume 6.

Tee hee hee! ♡
WELCOME HOME...
...MY KYO-KUN!

SLAM!
THE DOOR CLOSED?!
KYO-KUN, DEAR, WHAT'S WRONG?!
KYO-KUN?!
rattle rattle
YEAH, IT'S CLOSED! AND IT WON'T EVER OPEN AGAIN!!
KY-KY...
IT'LL TAKE MORE THAN A DOOR TO STOP HER...
KYO-KUN?!
*She hit her head
Just now, I heard a "slam" sound...

OPEN IT!
.....
.....
Then!
IN THAT CASE, DON'T COME!!
HUH?
I DON'T HAVE ANY BUSINESS.
WELL?! WHAT DO YOU WANT?
TELL ME YOUR BUSINESS AND LET'S GET THIS OVER WITH!!

WHY NOT.....?
CAN'T I COME TO SEE YOU WHEN I WANT TO?
I DON'T WANT TO SEE YOU!!
KYO-KUN...
YOU'RE SO CRUEL...
YOU'RE SO CRUEL, EVEN THOUGH...
KAGURA-SA...
EVEN THOUGH I LOVE YOU SOOOO MUCH!!
WOULD YOU HURRY UP AND FIGURE OUT THAT THAT'S *WHY* I DON'T WANT TO SEE YOU?!

ポイ
カリ
...OH.
SHI~~
GU~~
RE~~
ドオン...
HE'S TRYING TO GET RID OF HER TACTFULLY ...
SHII-CHAN, YOU SAY THE NICEST THINGS!
Kyahh
HEY! WAIT A MINUTE! WHAT DO YOU MEAN "LEND"?!
I'LL LEND HIM TO YOU, KAGURA.
WHY DON'T YOU TAKE HIM ON A DATE OR SOMETHING?

I'M NOT GOING!!
GROCERIES? YUP, YUP, WE'LL GO!
UH... UM...
THEN...
NN? REALLY?
I'M NOT GOING! FIRST OF ALL, I HAVE NO REASON TO GO OUTSIDE!!
THEN, TOHRU-KUN, WHY NOT ASK THEM TO BUY GROCERIES FOR DINNER?
EH?
I SAID, I'M--
...I HOPE I'M NOT IMPOSING, BUT COULD YOU DO IT?
...THEN...
All right!!
IT'S A DATE!!
HAVE A FUN BATTLE. ♡

WE JUST NEED TO GIVE KAGURA A LITTLE ALONE TIME WITH KYO, THEN SHE'LL SETTLE DOWN, RIGHT?
And she won't break my house.
KAGURA COULD STAND TO LET UP...
...A LITTLE.
EH?
"OPERATION: GET RID OF HER" IS A SUCCESS.
phew!
I KNEW IT.
...THAT LATELY, AS BEST SHE CAN, SHE'S BEEN TRYING TO GIVE HIM...
...SOME SPACE.
...SHE MIGHT ACTUALLY BE LET-TING UP SOME.
I THINK...
I COULD TELL...
I COULD SEE THAT SHE WAS REALLY HOLDING BACK...
...THE URGE TO SEE HIM EVERY DAY.

BUT IF KEEPING ALL HER FEELINGS PENT UP IS GOING TO CAUSE HER TO EXPLODE, MAYBE IT WOULD BE BETTER FOR HER TO COME EVERY DAY.
AND SHE WOULDN'T BREAK THE HOUSE.
I love my tea!
INDEED.
I'M GOING TO TAKE SOME MONEY FROM KYO'S BANK ACCOUNT AS A FINE.
Kagura, too.
I SEE. YOU NOTICED THAT, SO THAT'S WHY YOU GAVE HER...
...THE SHOPPING LIST.
IT'S ALMOST AS IF SHE KNOWS SOMETHING...
EH... UH...!
THE MAIN HOUSE PUTS MONEY INTO THEM EACH MONTH.
OH, REALLY?
I SEE...
HUH? OH, YES.
YUKI-KUN HAS ONE, TOO.
KYO-KUN HAS A BANK ACCOUNT?

.....
IT'S FUNNY.
AFTER ALL THIS TIME...
...THERE'S STILL SO MUCH I DON'T KNOW ABOUT THEM.
EH ?!
NO, I COULDN'T POSSIBLY--!
UH... UM...
UM...
I SHOULD ...UH... START THE LAUNDRY!
DON'T BOTHER. I THINK IT WILL START RAINING AGAIN SOON.
MORE IMPORTANTLY, YOU DON'T OFTEN GET THE OPPORTUNITY, TOHRU-KUN, SO WHY DON'T YOU GO ON A DATE WITH YUKI-KUN?

C'MON.
LET'S GO ON A DATE.
THAT IS, IF YOU DON'T MIND THE USUAL PLACE.
blush
BUT...
...IF THE DAY COMES WHEN I'M ALLOWED TO KNOW THEIR SECRETS...
...OKAY
...I WANT TO BE THE KIND OF PERSON WHO CAN ACCEPT THEM FOR WHO THEY ARE.

*nabe: hot pot; stew

mutter
.....
.....
KYO-KUN...
THAT'S NONE OF YOUR DAMN BUSINESS!!
SHUT UP!!
MUTTER CHATTER MUTTER
OW OW OW W!
YELLING AT A GIRL IN PUBLIC IS THE WORST THING YOU CAN DO!!

whisper whisper
whisper
OHH, OHH, KYO-KUN! THIS IS SO EMBARRASSING!
HERE. LET'S GO OVER THERE.
NORMALLY, PEOPLE WOULD AVOID ME.
I–!
……
……
WHY...
WHY DO YOU... CARE SO MUCH ABOUT ME ANYWAY?
KEEP THEIR DISTANCE...
KYO-KUN...
YOU DON'T KNOW...
IT'S WEIRD.
NORMALLY ...

THAT TIME...
YOU DON'T KNOW...
THAT'S WHY I...
.....
THAT'S WHY YOU'D WHAT?
.....
YOU WOULD CRY IF I TOLD YOU, KYO-KUN.
So it's a secret!
HUH?
NOW IT'S TIME FOR CHECKOUT.
HEY... WHAT IS IT?
C'MON. LET'S GO, KYO-KUN.
HEY!

LET'S HOLD HANDS ON THE WAY HOME. ♡
NOT A CHANCE.
tee hee
UH-OH.
IT LOOKS LIKE IT'S GOING TO RAIN AGAIN.
SHE'S NOT GOING TO TELL ME...
WHY NOT, WHY NOT?! WE USED TO HOLD HANDS ALL THE TIME!
YEAH...! WHEN WE WERE LIKE THREE OR FOUR!!
KYO-KUN!!
YOU'RE SO COLD...
chatter
chatter
chatter
.....!
I JUST HAVE TO HOLD YOUR HAND, RIGHT?! FINE!
tremble tremble
HERE!!

"NORMALLY...
...PEOPLE WOULD AVOID ME, KEEP THEIR DISTANCE."
HAVEN'T YOU REALIZED?
BUT ONLY HALFWAY, OKAY?!
.....
Okay!!

IT'S YOU...
...WHO DOES THAT, KYO-KUN.
Okay, Kagura-neechan!
Kyo-chan, let's go play!
Okay!

I WONDER IF KYO-KUN AND KAGURA-SAN WILL BE ALL RIGHT.
IF HE FAINTS, KAGURA WILL CARRY HIM HOME.
OH...
!
bump
AH...!
IT STARTED RAINING AGAIN.
?
I--
I'M SORR...
.....
?
IS SOMETHING WRONG...?

HE'S BACK...
HUH?
DO YOU KNOW HIM?
CUT IT OUT!!
.....?
KYO...
I HELD YOUR HAND THIS LONG. ISN'T THAT ENOUGH?!
YOU KNOW I HATE PEOPLE CLINGING TO ME!!
I KNOW, BUT THAT'S NO FUN!

*shishou: a martial arts master

YOU'RE LOOKING WELL...
...KYO.

People say to use everything...

Like pictures that you can only see online and stuff. Like Momiji, I put a lot of my own preferences into Kisa. It's really fun to draw her. I'm a real girly-girl at heart, so I would have liked to try wearing flowy dresses or maid outfits at least once, but it looks like that dream will go unfulfilled (laugh). Too bad.

Chapter 32

People say to use...

It's a rough sketch, so Mine's maid outfit is too plain. I'm sorry. Next time I'll draw it more seriously. (Huh?) The outfit Aaya is wearing was mostly designed by Aaya and made by Mine.

ULTRA-SPECIAL BLAH BLAH BLAH 2

There are those who think, "I don't need them to love everything about me..." And there are others who think that, "I want them to love everything." Both are valid points of view. I really can't say one way is better than the other. Both exist. Kyo is the former.

*shihan: another word for master or instructor.

Fruits Basket 6 Part 2:

A lot of people have told me, "It's okay to talk about games!" I'm glad. And so, without delay... (laugh) I finally finished *PERSONA 2: INNOCENT SIN.* (I had stopped in the middle.) I stopped right before the last boss, like with the first game. I wonder if it's inevitable...? For me, it is. I really liked Ginko. She was so cute when she said, "Aiya~" and stuff. Sadly, my Playstation is on its last legs, so during the ending song, it started skipping (laugh). Talk about Aiya~. Letting the credits go without sound... I'm playing *ETERNAL PUNISHMENT* on my PS2. (laugh)

(*INNOCENT SIN* and *ETERNAL PUNISHMENT* are both sequels to the sleeper hit RPG *PERSONA*. Only *ETERNAL PUNISHMENT* was released in the U.S. -ed.)

*ohisashiburi: The reason everyone is saying "It's been a long time," is because in Japan, there is a ritual phrase, "ohisashiburi," which is used when greeting someone you haven't seen in a while. It's similar to the way Japanese folk always say "Okaeri" (welcome home) when someone comes home, or "itadakimasu" (thanks for the food) before eating.

AH...!
I SEE...
TOHRU-SAN...
MAY I CALL YOU THAT?
AH!
Y-yes!! PLEASED TO MEET YOU! I-I'M TOHRU HONDA!
EH?
HUH?
TOHRU-KUN...
...THIS IS KAZUMA SOHMA-DONO.
AT THE SAME TIME HE WAS KYO-KUN'S SHISHOU ...
...HE TAUGHT MARTIAL ARTS TO YUKI, KAGURA, HAA-KUN AND THE OTHERS.
I SEE.
SO YOU'RE THE YOUNG LADY...

RUMOR IS, YOU KNOW THE SECRET...
...OF THE ZODIAC CURSE.
.....
Y-
YES!
.....
I SEE...
.....
.....?

YOU HAVEN'T SEEN HIM SINCE YOU TRAINED IN THE MOUNTAINS, RIGHT?
AREN'T YOU HAPPY TO SEE HIM AGAIN?
I–
GASP!
KYO-KUN.
WHY DON'T YOU STOP HIDING AND SAY HELLO?
C'mon, c'mon.
.....!!

COULD YOU DIRECT ME TO KYO'S ROOM, PLEASE?
AH! UM... IT'S AT THE END OF THE HALL ON THE RIGHT ON THE SECOND FLOOR... H-HERE, I'LL SHOW YOU...
NO, THAT'S ALL I NEED.
すっ
!
AH...
KYO-KU...?
STOMP STOMP STOMP STOMP STOMP
?
WHAT'S LIKE WHO?
tee hee
YOU KNOW, IT'S JUST LIKE KYO-KUN.
UH-HUH!
THAT'S SO LIKE HIM.
step step
tee hee hee
heh heh

...IN FRONT OF YUN-CHAN.
whisper whisper
whisper
ESPECIALLY ...
...BUT HE DOESN'T WANT TO SHOW IT.
KYO-KUN IS ACTUALLY REALLY HAPPY...

clack
KYO?
I'M COMING IN.
SHISHOU.
...OH, I SEE YOU'VE BEEN DOING A LOT OF READING.
!
They're Shigure's books.

I'M SORRY...
...FOR MY DISRESPECT.
IT'S ALL RIGHT.
I UNDERSTAND.
.....
YOU'RE ALWAYS THE SAME IN FRONT OF YUKI.

.....
WELCOME BACK!
WELCOME BACK, SHISHOU!!

I'M GLAD TO SEE YOU, TOO.
SO...
...IS SHISHOU-SAN NOT ONE OF THE ZODIAC?

?
NO.
BUT HE IS ONE OF THE PEOPLE ON THE "INSIDE."
THEY SAY THAT THE ONE WHO WAS THE CAT BEFORE KYO-KUN WAS SHIHAN'S GRANDFATHER.

THAT'S WHY...
...SHIHAN MIGHT BE THE ONE WHO CAN BEST RELATE TO KYO-KUN.

...AS IF HE WERE HIS REAL FATHER.
BUT IT'S LIKE SHIHAN CARES FOR KYO-KUN EVEN MORE THAN THAT.
HE WATCHED OVER KYO-KUN SO THAT HE WOULDN'T GET HURT...

HIS REAL...
...FATHER...
SO NOW YOUR TRAINING JOURNEY IS OVER?
YES. I CAN'T AFFORD TO BE AWAY FROM THE DOJO ANY LONGER.
ALL RIGHT, THEN!
I CAN GO BACK TO THE DOJO TOO, RIGHT?!
YOU PROMISED BEFORE YOU LEFT!

"WHEN I COME BACK, COME STAY WITH ME AGAIN."
"NOW WE MUST PART WAYS UNTIL THAT DAY."
I'M SORRY...
YOU ARE TO CONTINUE TO LIVE HERE.
WHETHER YOUR COMING TO LIVE WITH THAT GIRL...
...IS A COINCIDENCE OR AN INEVITABILITY ...
...IT HAS A HEALING EFFECT ON YOU.
SHISHOU.
WHAT...? YOU'RE BREAKING YOUR PROMISE?
YOU'RE NOT SCARED OF AKITO, TOO, ARE YOU?
NO.
I HAVE COME TO THE CONCLUSION THAT THIS IS THE BEST ENVIRONMENT FOR YOU.

I...
...NEVER ASKED TO BE HEALED.
I HATE IT HERE.
I FEEL LIKE I'M DROWNING!
DROWNING IN LUKEWARM WATER OR SOMETHING. SOMETIMES...
SOMETIMES, IT GETS SO BAD...
I HATE IT HERE.
...I CAN'T STAND IT.

KYO...
SHIHAN IS GOING TO STAY HERE TONIGHT, RIGHT?
IT'S NOT THAT YOU "HATE" IT.
THAT'S NOT...
... REALLY TRUE, IS IT?
I'M STAYING, TOO! ♡
SHII-CHAN SAID IT'S OKAY! ♡

WHERE SHOULD WE LAY OUT SHISHOU-SAN'S FUTON?
MAYBE SHIGURE-SAN'S ROOM...?
WHAT THE HELL?! GO HOME!
EEHH ?!
I WONDER WHERE SHIGURE-SAN FINDS ROOM TO SLEEP...?
LET'S NOT. DEFINITELY NOT.
I wouldn't wish that on anyone.
The Sea of Decay returns!
Around there somewhere
WHY NOT JUST MAKE HIM SLEEP HERE IN THE LIVING ROOM?
It's not like he's a kid.
HAAH ?!
I'LL GO ASK!
HEY!
YOU'RE RIGHT! THAT WOULD BE BEST.
hmm...
I WONDER IF KYO-KUN'S ROOM WOULD BE THE BEST?

THE TWO OF YOU MUST HAVE A LOT TO TALK ABOUT, KYO-KUN.
...I DON'T.
AH!
OH YEAH. UM... IF I COULD...
SOMEDAY I WOULD REALLY LIKE TO SEE...
...A MATCH BETWEEN YOU AND SHISHOU-SAN!
Honda-san, what should I do with this?
Ah! Yes, that's ...

THINGS MIGHT GET NOISY.
I APOLOGIZE IN ADVANCE.
TONIGHT ...
...I'M GOING TO TAKE IT OFF.
...I THOUGHT THAT, FOR HER, HE MIGHT OPEN HIS HEART.
AND THAT SHE, IN TURN, MIGHT ACCEPT IT.
...IS TO DO THIS NOW.
AND THE ONLY WAY TO SEE IF THIS IS THE CASE...
ISN'T THAT A LITTLE RASH?
WHAT MADE YOU COME TO THAT DECISION SO SUDDENLY?
TODAY...
TODAY, WHEN I SAW...
...THAT GIRL'S FACE...
.....

SO EVEN YOU, KAZUMA-DONO, ARE GOING TO ENTRUST EVERY-THING...
...TO HER?
BUT...
...YOU HAVE NO GUARANTEE THAT THIS WILL SUCCEED.
EVEN IF SHE DOES ACCEPT HIM, IT'S POSSIBLE THAT KYO WILL REJECT HER.
THIS TIME, THERE IS THE POSSIBILITY THAT KYO WILL BREAK.
HE MIGHT COME TO HATE EVEN YOU.
HE MAY NEVER...
...SMILE AGAIN.
WITH SO MUCH AT STAKE...
...ARE YOU STILL WILLING TO TAKE THE ONE IN TEN-THOUSAND CHANCE?
"AW, MAN!"

"NNNN... IT LOOKS LIKE I STILL NEED A LOT OF TRAINING, TOO."
"HA HA!"
"LOOK AT IT! HOW THE HECK COULD YOU SCREW UP SOMETHING SO SIMPLE, SHISHOU?
YOU REALLY ARE NO GOOD AT THIS."
EXCUSE ME, BUT TONIGHT MAY I BORROW SOME OF YOUR TIME?
EVEN SO...
EVEN SO, I WANT TO TAKE THE CHANCE...
...ON HER.

SHISHOU... WELL...
DO WE REALLY HAVE TO GO OUTSIDE TO TALK?
YOU KNOW HOW I GET ON DAYS LIKE THIS.
?
BECAUSE THIS GIRL MAY BE THE ONE.
MY GRAND-FATHER WAS THE SAME WAY.
I UNDERSTAND HE OFTEN GOT SICK ON RAINY DAYS.
IS IT BECAUSE YOU ARE POSSESSED BY THE CAT?
IS IT BECAUSE THE VENGEFUL SPIRIT OF YOUR TRUE FORM HATES THE RAIN?
PLEASE ...
PLEASE... FOR KYO.

I ACCEPT THAT MY LIFE IS WORTHLESS BECAUSE I WAS BORN THE CAT!
.....!
AND IT'S THE RAT'S--
I DO ACCEPT IT!
drip
drop
drip
IF YOU DO NOT FULLY ACCEPT YOUR TRUE FORM SOON...
...YOU WILL NEVER BE ABLE TO PROGRESS.
--IT'S HIS FAULT...
...BECAUSE HE STARTED ALL OF THIS!!

ARE YOU GOING TO CONTINUE TO LIVE THAT WAY...
...EVEN NOW?
"IF I DIE TOO, YOU'LL BE SATISFIED, RIGHT?!"
YOU HAVEN'T CHANGED...
"IT'S HIS FAULT! IT'S ALL HIS FAULT!"
STOPPING YOUR EARS, CLOSING YOUR EYES...
SHUTTING YOURSELF OFF FROM THE WORLD WITH YOUR HATRED OF YUKI.
IS THAT THE ONLY WAY YOU WANT TO LIVE?
"THEN YOU'LL BE SATISFIED, RIGHT?"
"I'LL KILL HIM AND THEN I'LL KILL MYSELF!"

AND...
...IS THAT THE WAY YOU WANT TO DIE?
COMPLETELY ALONE.
LIKE MY GRANDFATHER.
YOU SAID YOURSELF...
...THAT YOU HATE IT HERE.
BUT THAT'S NOT IT... IT'S NOT THAT YOU HATE IT.
IT'S THAT YOU'RE AFRAID. YOU WANT TO RUN AWAY.

...THE TRUTH IS, YOU DO NOT WANT HER TO KNOW YOUR **TRUE FORM.**
YOU ARE AFRAID OF LOSING HER IF SHE FINDS OUT.
THE WARM FEELING YOU COMPARED TO "DROWNING IN LUKEWARM WATER"...
...YOU KNOW THAT IT WILL **HEAL** YOU.
BUT...
YOU ARE JUST TRYING TO RUN AWAY FROM THAT UNCERTAINTY.

WILL YOU LOSE HER, OR WILL YOU NOT?
I WILL HELP YOU FIND THE ANSWER.
YOU'RE WRON--
YOU LEAVE ME NO OTHER CHOICE.
I WILL TAKE AWAY YOUR MEANS OF ESCAPE.
KYO...
...DISCOVER FOR YOUR-SELF...
...WHETHER OR NOT YOUR BIRTHRIGHT REALLY MAKES YOU "WORTHLESS."

IT'S ALL RIGHT...
I LOVE YOU, LITTLE ONE.

DON'T LOOK...
"I WON'T LET ANYONE SEE YOU."
"NO ONE LOOK...
DON'T LOOK...
...AT MY CHILD.

DON'T LOOK AT ME!!
"IT'S DISGUSTING."

Chapter 33
"AND WHAT'S THAT SMELL?
"HIS BODY'S ALL WARPED AND UGLY."
"HE SMELLS TERRIBLE."
"IS THIS...
...THE CAT SPIRIT'S..."
"THIS IS KYO'S TRUE FORM?"
"IT SMELLS LIKE SOME-THING'S ROTTING."

"...TRUE FORM?"

.....
KYO...
...KUN

"IT'S DISGUSTING."
!!

SHE SAW ME...
SHE SAW ME...
SHE SAW ME...
IT'S OVER!
IT'S OVER. EVERYTHING ...
IT'S ALL...
...HOPELESS.

.....
...OTHER FORM.
THAT...
...IS WHAT HE HAS BEEN HIDING. THE CAT'S...
ONLY THOSE POSSESSED BY THE CAT CHANGE INTO THAT GROTESQUE FORM.
.....
WERE YOU...
...DISGUSTED?
DID YOU THINK HE WAS FRIGHTENING?

WHAT SHOULD I DO?
I CAN'T BREATHE!
BUT...
BUT...
WHAT IN THE WORLD SHOULD I DO?
WHAT'S HAPPENING?
IT'S TO MUCH FOR ME TO HANDLE...
Kuh!
GAGH...!
cough
cough
cough

WHAT AN INCREDIBLY HORRIBLE SMELL!
IT'S LIKE THE STENCH OF ROTTING FLESH IS EVERY-WHERE...
EVEN VOMITING DOESN'T MAKE IT BETTER...
BLEH!
gag
UH.....
GUAGH!
だんっ
KYO-KUN'S OTHER FORM.
I'VE NEVER SMELLED ANYTHING LIKE IT.
I'VE NEVER SEEN ANYTHING LIKE IT.
THAT WAS KYO-KUN...

WILL YOU...
...HEAL HIM?

"WHAT'S WRONG? DID SOME-THING HAPPEN AGAIN?"
"KYO..."
"DID AKITO SAY SOME-THING?"
"IT'S ALL RIGHT."
"MOMMY LOVES YOU."
STOP IT!!
STOP...

crack
.....
IT'S TOO MUCH...
TOO MUCH!
KYO-KUN...
huff
huff
huff
.....
KYO...
...KUN...
STAY AWAY!!

Fruits Basket 6 Part 3:

I'm still in the middle of *SUMMON NIGHT*. But *HARUKANARU TOKI NO NAKA DE* was amazing. This might be the fastest I've ever completed a game. I think the captures I made might have even been helpful to someone. (Don't flatter yourself. They weren't.) And again, my Playstation's in bad shape, so there were sound issues. Such a tragedy... Still, I played as if entranced. I love Tomomasa-san and Inori-kun. (Those two don't match, Takaya.) I can't wait to play *ANGELIQUE TROIS*. There should be a lot more of them! I love Love-sim games! They fill my heart with joy. Even when a game isn't a love-sim, I like it when designers throw in a little romance. Yay!

I'M DISGUSTING, AREN'T I?!
I'M SICKENING, AREN'T I?!
WHY DON'T YOU LEAVE ME ALONE?!
I DON'T WANT YOUR PITY!!
I'M BEGGING YOU...
PLEASE, STOP.
KYO-KU...
KYO-KUN... BUT...
huff
huff
huff
BUT I...
"BECAUSE I AM YOUR..."
DON'T TOUCH ME!!!

STOP...
I'M GOING TO MAKE YOU MISERABLE!
ドザ
GET LOST!

GET LOST!!
YOU DRIVE ME CRAZY!
I CAN'T STAND TO LOOK AT YOU!!
NEXT TIME I'LL CUT YOUR FACE TO PIECES!!
...I'LL MAKE IT SO BAD, I'LL HURT HER SO MUCH...
IF I'M GOING TO LOSE HER ANYWAY...
...THAT IT COULDN'T POSSIBLY HURT ANY MORE!

THAT SHE'LL NEVER WANT TO LOOK BACK!
I'LL MAKE IT SO BAD...
...THAT SHE'LL NEVER FEEL SORRY FOR ME AGAIN.
"AKITO'S WRONG. YOU ARE HUMAN, LIKE EVERYONE ELSE."
HAVING THIS FATE FORCED ON ME.
BEING MISERABLE...
I HATE THIS!
LOSING HER, BEING PITIED...
"YOU'RE JUST UNDER AN EVIL SPELL FOR A LITTLE WHILE THAT MAKES YOU TURN INTO THAT."

"YOU'RE MY SON AND I'M SO PROUD OF YOU."
THAT'S NOT TRUE.
IF IT WAS, WHY DIDN'T YOU EVER LET ME GO OUTSIDE?
"YOU'RE SO CUTE, I WON'T LET ANYONE ELSE SEE YOU."
YOU WERE ASHAMED, WEREN'T YOU?
NO, I LOVE YOU.
YOU REALLY WERE SCARED, WEREN'T YOU?
THAT'S WHY EVERY DAY, DOZENS OF TIMES ...
... YOU CHECKED TO MAKE SURE MY BEADS HADN'T COME OFF, RIGHT?
"AS PROOF, LOOK... YOU CHANGED RIGHT BACK."
"IT'S ALL RIGHT."
"I'M NOT SCARED A BIT."
THAT'S A LIE.

"IF IT WOULD HELP YOU, YOUR MOTHER...
...WOULD DIE FOR YOU."
DON'T FORCE THAT LOVE ON ME!
I DON'T NEED IT... I DON'T NEED IT!
YOUR MOTHER LOVED YOU MORE THAN ANYONE!!
I DON'T CARE IF YOU FIND ME SCARY...
WHY DO YOU ALWAYS SAY THINGS LIKE THAT?
YOU WON'T EVEN ACKNOWLEDGE THE REAL ME...
STOP IT!!
I...I JUST...
...MORE THAN ANYTHING ELSE...
...SO WHY ARE YOU ALWAYS ACTING LIKE YOU LOVE ME SO MUCH?

...I WANTED US TO BE TOGETHER.
?!
YOU HAVE TO GO BACK.
BACK HOME.
...LET'S GO BACK.
YOU...

I'M WORRIED THAT KYO-KUN WON'T COME HOME...
...EVER AGAIN.
YOU JUST HAVE TO...
I COULDN'T BEAR IT IF YOU DON'T!
DON'T YOU GET IT?!
LET GO...
STOP IT!
NO! I DON'T GET IT!
.....
I'M... SCARED...
"DID YOU THINK HE WAS FRIGHTENING?"
RIGHT NOW... KYO-KUN...
...LISTENING TO YOUR VOICE, IT'S LIKE IT'S NOT YOU.
I'VE NEVER SEEN ANYTHING LIKE IT.
IT'S SCARY...

...KYO-KUN TO SUFFER ALONE.
WHEN THINGS GET TOUGH...
...WHEN YOU'RE SCARED, WHEN YOU'RE WEAK...
...I WANT YOU TO TELL ME.
I WANT YOU TO LET ME CARE ABOUT YOU.
I WANT TO BE TOGETHER.
FROM NOW ON...
...JUST LIKE YOU LISTENED TO MY COMPLAINTS, KYO-KUN...
...I WANT YOU TO LET ME LISTEN TO YOURS.
I JUST DON'T WANT...
BUT...
BUT...
BUT FROM NOW ON...
...I WANT TO UNDERSTAND EVERYTHING...

"TOGETHER."
I WANT US TO LIVE...
...EAT MEALS, STUDY...
...SHARE OUR TROUBLES ...
...LIKE WE DID BEFORE...
TOGETHER.
I WANT TO STAY TOGETHER!!
BUT DIDN'T...
I'M BEING...
...KYO-KUN TELL ME--
...SO SELFISH.

Y...
YOU...
YOU DON'T HAVE TO...LOVE EVERYTHING.
"IT'S OKAY TO BE SELFISH ONCE IN A WHILE."
DIDN'T YOU SAY THAT TO ME?
IT'S OKAY...
...IF YOU WERE SCARED.
IT'S OKAY...

YOU WOULDN'T EVEN THINK ABOUT ME...
BUT, MOM...
YOU ALWAYS TOLD ME THAT YOU LOVED ME, BUT YOU WOULDN'T EVEN LOOK AT ME.
BECAUSE BEING SCARED...
...IS PROOF THAT YOU'RE ACTUALLY LOOKING AT MY UGLINESS.
...ALL ALONG.
TO HAVE SOMEONE TO SHARE MY WORRIES WITH.
DID YOU REALLY THINK IT WAS ENOUGH TO JUST TALK LIKE YOU LOVED ME?
THIS IS WHAT I WANTED...
LET'S GO ON LIVING...
BUT EVEN SO...
IT'S OKAY IF YOU DON'T LOVE MY HIDEOUS SELF.
IT'S OKAY IF YOU'RE SCARED.
...TOGETHER.

I ALWAYS ASSUMED...
IT SOUNDS SO STUPID.
...THAT NO ONE WOULD EVER...
...UNDERSTAND ME.

I NEVER THOUGHT...
...TOHRU.
TOHRU...!
...I'D HEAR THOSE WORDS.

KYO-KUN...?
WHY...
...WOULD SOMEONE LIKE YOU...
...STAY NEAR ME...
...AND CRY FOR ME?
JUST LIKE THAT...
...THE UGLY EMOTIONS INSIDE ME...
...THE MUD-COVERED ANXIETY...
ONE BY ONE, YOU MELT THEM AWAY.

HOW CAN I ASK FOR THAT?
I DON'T...
... DESERVE SOMETHING LIKE THAT.
YOU ENDED UP NEAR ME BY MISTAKE.
THIS TIME WILL BE DIFFERENT.
THIS TIME...
...I WANT TO CARE FOR YOU.

I DON'T WANT US TO BE APART.
HOW CAN I ASK FOR THAT?

Chapter 34

"IF ONLY SHE HADN'T HAD THAT CAT CHILD."
"POOR THING."
"I GUESS IT WAS SO HARD ON HER HAVING THE CAT AS A SON THAT SHE KILLED HERSELF."
"BUT NO ONE KNOWS FOR SURE."
"FROM WHAT I HEAR, IT SEEMS LIKE SUICIDE."
"AND HE'S THE ONE WHO PUSHED HER TO SUICIDE."
"EVEN THOUGH HIS MOTHER DIED."
"THE BOY DOESN'T EVEN CRY."
... SHUT UP.

THAT'S RIGHT.
IT'S NOT MY FAULT!!
IT'S NOT MY FAULT!!
SHUT UP!

I KNOW.

PLEASED TO MEET YOU.
I AM KAZUMA SOHMA.
IT'S NOT MY FAULT...
IT'S NOT MY...
IT'S NOT MY FAULT!!
!!
IT'S ALL RIGHT.
IT'S ALL RIGHT.
I KNOW.

I MAY NOT LOOK LIKE IT...
...BUT I'M ACTUALLY AN INSTRUCTOR AT A KARATE DOJO.
IF YOU'RE INTERESTED, YOU SHOULD TRY IT.
THIS MAN...
KYO...?
WON'T YOU COME STAY WITH ME?
"HEY– LOOK AT KYO."
WHY DID HE WANT TO TAKE ME IN?
I DIDN'T KNOW IF IT WAS SYMPATHY OR IF HE WAS FOLLOWING SOMEONE'S ORDERS.

"KAZUMA-KUN REALLY TOOK THE BOY IN."
"I KNOW THAT KID MUST HAVE BEEN HARD ON HIS FATHER, BUT I WOULDN'T WISH HIM ON POOR KAZUMA-KUN."
"TELL ME ABOUT IT! HE'S SO YOUNG. OF ALL THE THINGS..."
I DIDN'T REALIZE IT THEN, BUT...
?!
?!
FROM NOW ON...
...YOU WILL HAVE TO BREATHE THE AIR OF HIGHER PLACES.
?!

HE TOOK MY HAND...
Wh-wh-what is that?
It's a train.
T-train.
...HE WAS THE FIRST ONE TO SHOW ME THE "OUTSIDE" WORLD.
...AND STAYED BY MY SIDE.
You must also train your spirit.
Patience.
Sitting straight

Ah ha ha!
THAT MAY BE RIGHT.
BUT...
...NONE OF MY STUDENTS WILL CALL ME THAT.

H...
EH?
HEY, YOU'RE A SHISHOU, RIGHT?
ON TV THEY WERE CALLING A KARATE INSTRUCTOR "SHISHOU," SO YOU'RE A SHISHOU, RIGHT?

HE HELPED ME.
Ah ha ha!
.....
Ah ha ha!
SHI...
Ha ha ...
SHISHOU ...
WELCOME HOME...
...KYO!
SHISHOU HELPED ME SO MUCH.
SO MUCH THAT...

...THAT I WISH SHISHOU WAS MY REAL FATHER.

HIS RAISING ME MAY HAVE JUST BEEN SYMPATHY AND KINDNESS ...
WOULD HE LAUGH OR LOOK TROUBLED?
OR WOULD HE BE SPEECH-LESS?
I WONDER HOW HE'D REACT IF I TOLD HIM THAT.

"I UNDERSTAND HE'S JUST YOUR FOSTER FATHER...
...BUT HOW ON EARTH DID HE RAISE YOU?"

"ALL THEY DID WAS TEASE YOU ABOUT YOUR HAIR COLOR."
"YOUR FATHER IS ON HIS WAY HERE."
clack

...HIS SHARE OF SCORN.
...BUT HE CERTAINLY HAD TO PUT UP WITH...
"WHY DO YOU TRY TO SOLVE THINGS WITH VIOLENCE?"

PEOPLE WOULD SAY THINGS SO TERRIBLE YOU'D WANT TO PUKE.
THINGS THAT WOULDN'T HAVE BEEN SAID IF IT WEREN'T FOR ME.
SHISHOU ACCEPTED IT ALL...
...AND RAISED ME IN SPITE OF IT.
SHISHOU ISN'T MY DAD!!
"I CAN'T BELIEVE HE WILLINGLY TOOK IN THE CAT."
"IS SOMETHING WRONG WITH KAZUMA-KUN TOO?"
IF I HURT HIM...
.....
NO WAY!
SO WHAT MORE DO I WANT?

I DON'T WANT YOU TO BE MY DAD...
DON'T EVER TREAT SHISHOU AND ME LIKE FATHER AND SON AGAIN!!
I DON'T WANT PEOPLE TO SAY BAD THINGS ANYMORE.
I DON'T WANT TO BE ANYONE'S BURDEN.
...IF IT'S GOING TO HURT YOU.
daze
.....
.....
!
カリ
ッ

Fruits Basket 6 Part 4:

As I'm writing this, FF9 still hasn't come out. Just a little longer. Finally, the most dangerous game... The game that I will put everything aside for, even eating... No, if I get too hungry, I will eat. (So you will eat!) There are things in the world whose power to draw you in is strong. Things that fill you with anticipation are the strongest of all. Like Square-san's games. Y'know? You think, "I'm sleepy... I'm sleepy, but... I have to know what happens next!" Goodness gracious. And *GRANDIA 2* is coming out! I'm so happy I could scream. And a Dreamcast version of *SAKURA TAISEN* is on its way, so I scream even more. Aahh, there aren't enough hours in the day! (laugh)

RUN
RUN
RUN
RUN
SLAM
WHA...
WHAT DID YOU SAY?
.....!
"I WILL TAKE AWAY YOUR MEANS OF ESCAPE."
"KYO...
...DISCOVER FOR YOURSELF WHETHER OR NOT YOUR BIRTHRIGHT REALLY MAKES YOU 'WORTHLESS.'"
WHY DID HE GO HOME...
...WITHOUT SAYING ANYTHING?

"YOU WILL NEVER BE ABLE TO PROGRESS."
WHY?
HE DIDN'T EVEN GIVE ME A CHANCE...
...TO SAY A WORD OF THANKS!
I WILL BE FINE FROM HERE.
THANK YOU VERY MUCH.
AH...
UM... I REALLY THINK YOU SHOULD HAVE SAID SOME-THING TO KYO-KUN.
I KNOW IT'S NOT ANY OF MY BUSINESS... BUT...
THAT IS...

...WAS TO ATONE.
.....
THE REASON...
...I TOOK KYO IN...
.....
I DON'T KNOW.
MY GRAND-FATHER WAS POSSESSED BY THE CAT, JUST LIKE KYO IS.
AND I...
...WAS ONE OF THEM.
HE WAS ESTRANGED FROM HIS IMMEDIATE FAMILY, SLANDERED BY HIS RELATIVES.
THEY TREATED HIM VERY BADLY.

I ONLY MET MY GRANDFATHER ONCE.
"COME HERE, KAZUMA.
HAVE SOME CANDY."
I SAID SOME-THING...
...TERRIBLY CRUEL.
"I SEE..."
"I...
I DON'T WANT ANY!"
"IT'S CURSED!"
...JUST SMILED AT ME AND FORGAVE ME.
HE WAS SUCH A KIND PERSON.
MY GRAND-FATHER ...

MY GRAND-FATHER DIED, AND I GREW UP.
WHEN KYO WAS BORN...
...I SAW FIRST-HAND THE HARSH REALITY HE HAD TO FACE BECAUSE OF WHAT HE WAS BORN INTO. AND IT HIT ME.
HOW FOOLISH IT WAS...
...AND HOW CRUEL.
IT WAS NO DIFFERENT FROM US BACK THEN.
AND IT...
I ACTED EXACTLY THE SAME WAY.
AND SO I TOOK HIM IN TO ATONE FOR WHAT I'D DONE.
IT MAY HAVE STARTED ...
...FROM A SELFISH DESIRE TO EASE MY OWN GUILT...
.....
...HOW-EVER...
HOWEVER, SPENDING TIME WITH HIM...
...LIVING WITH HIM...
...BEFORE I KNEW IT...

I TREASURED HIM...
...WORRIED ABOUT HIM...
...WANTED HIM TO BE HAPPIER THAN ANYONE ELSE.
...I CAME TO LOVE HIM.
EVERY TIME I SAW HIM SMILE...
...THAT LOVE GREW.
I FELT LIKE...
...I HAD BECOME HIS FATHER.
BUT THIS TIME...
...I IGNORED HIS WILL AND TOOK HIS BEADS.
I FORCED MY ONE-SIDED FEELINGS ONTO HIM.
"SHISHOU ISN'T MY DAD!!"

...WHAT I COULD HAVE SAID.
I FORCED MY WILL ON HIM.
SAYING, "GOOD FOR YOU," WOULD HAVE BEEN TOO...

TOO SELFISH.
ANYWAY, I ONLY CREATED THE IMPETUS.
THE ONE WHO SAVED KYO...
...IS YOU.

BECAUSE YOU WERE THERE FOR HIM...
...KYO...

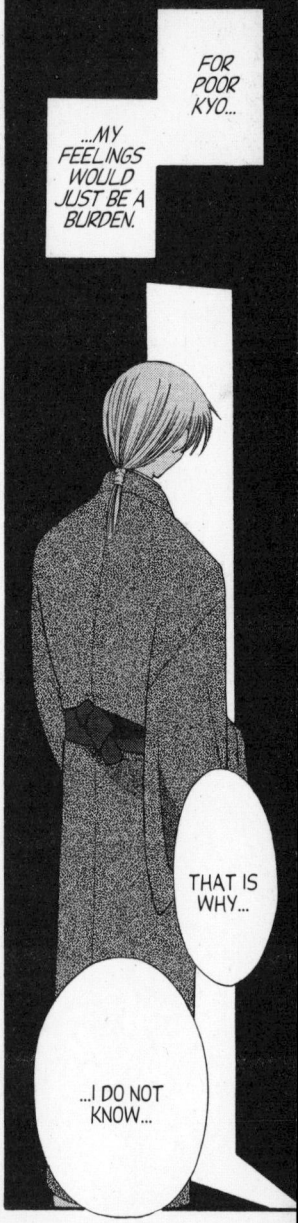
FOR POOR KYO...
...MY FEELINGS WOULD JUST BE A BURDEN.
THAT IS WHY...
...I DO NOT KNOW...

SHISHOU-SAN...
SHISHOU-SAN, WAS THAT...
...REALLY JUST YOUR WILL?
I DON'T KNOW WHY...
...BUT SOMEHOW...
...I HAVE A VERY WARM FEELING INSIDE.
SHISHOU-SAN... I DON'T PRETEND TO KNOW HOW YOU FEEL...
...BUT TO ME, RIGHT NOW, YOU SEEM...
...SHISHOU-SAN, YOU SEEM...
...VERY MUCH LIKE A FATHER.

SHISHOU!!
……
KYO-KU--
!

.....!
WHY--?!
KY...
WHY?!
WHY DID YOU LEAVE WITHOUT SAYING ANYTHING?!
HOW COULD YOU JUST...
...RUN AWAY LIKE THAT?!

KYO...
WHAT WAS IT?
OR ARE YOU...
ARE YOU...
...SICK OF ME?
DID YOU THINK I'D GET MAD OR SOMETHING?!

YOU SACRIFICED SO MUCH TO RAISE ME, AND I JUST ACTED LIKE A SPOILED KID.
WANTING TO GO BACK TO THE DOJO LIKE THAT...
USING YOU AS AN EXCUSE TO RUN AWAY... I'M SORRY.
ALL I EVER DO IS CAUSE YOU TROUBLE.
.....
I'M SORRY...
BUT--!
...WITHOUT HURTING ANYONE...
...AND WITHOUT BEING A BURDEN.
SOMEDAY I'LL BE ABLE TO STAND AND WALK ON MY OWN...
MAYBE I'M NOT PERFECT...
MAYBE I HAVE A LONG WAY TO GO. BUT SOMEDAY...
.....
.....
SHISHOU, YOU...
YOU...

...I'LL BE THE KIND OF GUY...
.....!
WHO CAN HOLD HIS HEAD HIGH.
SOMEDAY ...
...WHO'S WORTHY...
...OF CALLING YOU...

...MY DAD!!

WE TOOK THE LONG WAY, BUT NOW...
...I THINK WE JUST MIGHT BE ABLE...
...TO CONNECT.
...WE KEPT MISSING EACH OTHER.
ALL THIS TIME...

IT MUST BE...
?!
snap
.....
YOU'RE STILL...

KYO.
.....
TH...
...MY TROUBLE-SOME...
...SON.
...THAT'S NO REASON TO THROW ME!
IF YOU WERE NOT ABLE TO GUARD AGAINST THAT...
...THEN PERHAPS YOU'VE GOTTEN WEAKER?

.....
AH!
TOHRU!
EH?!
MY SHISHOU IS THE STRONGEST!
WERE YOU WATCHING?
EH? AH, YES!!
SEE?!
DIDN'T I TELL YOU?!

Y'KNOW, IT'S REALLY IRRITATING WHEN YOU KEEP REPEATING YOURSELF.
I'm no match for him anyway.
EH?!
...Yes.
Yes!
Yes!!

IT MUST BE...
...BECAUSE OF THIS PERSON.
ISN'T HE THE BEST?
URR...
BECAUSE YOU, TOHRU-SAN...
...WERE HERE FOR HIM.

Chapter 34

People say...

Shigure—he looks like he's worrying, but Shigure never worries. I look forward to drawing him more deeply. (With this and that...) No, but I like to draw all the characters. I might want to draw that soon! (laugh)

ULTRA-SPECIAL BLAH BLAH BLAH 3

Aaya is worrying about his brother in his own special way (laugh). Holding a crab claw... By the way, the colors are all secretly unified. There's no really deep meaning in it.

tug
.....
SO, YOU'RE GOING TO START GOING TO KAZUMA-DONO'S DOJO AGAIN?
BUT WHY JUST THREE DAYS A WEEK?
THAT'S ...
?
"THAT'S"?

DOES IT MATTER?! LEAVE ME ALONE!!
OHHH... SO DEFENSIVE! NOW YOU'VE MADE ME SUSPICIOUS.
TOHRU-KUN, DO YOU KNOW WHY?
EH?
GOOD MORNING.
STOP ALWAYS ASKING HER!
GOOD MORNING, YUKI-KUN!
WHAT ARE THEY YELLING ABOUT SO EARLY IN THE MORNING?
THOSE TWO.
bicker
squabble
That is...
THREE DAYS A WEEK SEEMS SUSPICIOUS, BUT STOP ASKING ME IS THE REASON... I THINK.
SO IT'S A STUPID ARGUMENT.
SHIGURE, WHY DO YOU HAVE TO ALWAYS...
...INTERROGATE PEOPLE LIKE THAT?!
ヒュッ
swoosh

CLACK
!
YOU'RE THROWING THEM AWAY?!
chuck

Fruits Basket 6 Part 5:

Ahh, I can't move my hand anymore... I have to go to the doctor. "VALKYRIE PROFILE is a wonderful game, isn't it?" I thought. No, oh how do I explain it, the system and everything... come to think of it, I don't really have anything to say about it. When Lucian dropped a broken crystal (it ended up broken), I got chills. That may not have anything to do with it, though. (laugh) Now that I think of it, I keep all the games I've beaten. All those jewel cases and cartridges, you know? They're taking up so much space it's not even funny! I don't know what to do with them. I just can't throw them away. It's a conundrum.

CAT.
PID
STU
snap
YOU
I COMMEND YOUR DISCIPLINE ...
YOU GIRLY MAN!!
HE'LL NEVER CHANGE!
AH!
KY...
YOU PISS ME OFF!! YOU REALLY PISS ME OFF!!
YOU ARE THE ONE PERSON I WILL HATE AND HATE AND HATE 'TIL THEY PUT ME IN MY GRAVE!
KYO-KU...

DUMBASS !!
GRAH!
"AAUGH, THINK WHATEVER YOU WANT, DAMMIT," RIGHT? SO PREDICTABLE.
STOMP STOMP STOMP
AH!
AH, UH, UM, BUT AT LEAST IT DIDN'T TURN INTO A FIGHT!
IT LOOKS LIKE IT WILL STILL BE A WHILE...
...BEFORE HE CAN MAKE THAT A REALITY.
THAT'S MY LINE.
I WILL KEEP HATING YOU...
...EVEN AFTER I'VE BEEN BURIED.

KAGURA-SAN.
SHE WAS THERE WHEN I WENT TO BED...
...BUT SHE WAS ALREADY GONE WHEN I WOKE UP AND I HAVEN'T SEEN HER SINCE.
...THAT I WAS ABLE TO LEARN ABOUT KYO-KUN'S FEELINGS...
...AND HIS RELATION-SHIP WITH SHISHOU-SAN.
BUT...
...THERE ARE STILL SOME THINGS ABOUT THAT NIGHT THAT LEFT ME ANXIOUS.
HONDA-SAN, HAVE YOU STARTED THINKING ABOUT FINALS YET?
EH...
EH?!
UH... WELL, UM...
not yet.
I'M VERY HAPPY...

AND THEN...
... THERE'S YUKI-KUN.
Ha ha ha
IT'S HARD TO TELL.
IT'S HARD TO TELL, BUT...
... YUKI-KUN SEEMS DEPRESSED SOMEHOW.
HONDA-SAN.

HE WAS ANNOYING, SO I LEFT HIM IN CLASS.
Oh...
Momiji-kun, takes some candy!
happy happy joy
Good for you, Momiji!!
Make sure to thank her!
HELLO, HATSUHARU-SAN!
YOU'RE NOT WITH MOMIJI-KUN TODAY?
HEY.
IS...YUKI AROUND?
AH... NO, IT SEEMS HE WENT SOME-WHERE.
IF YOU WANT, I COULD GIVE HIM A MESSAGE.
.....
IT'S NOT REALLY A MESSAGE...
WHEN I SAW HIM EARLIER, HE LOOKED TROUBLED.
IT'S HARD TO TELL, BUT...

THAT NIGHT ...
...MAYBE YUKI-KUN SAW...
...KYO'S TRUE FORM.
HE SEEMS DEPRESSED SOMEHOW.
AH...!
...I REALIZED...
...MAY... MAYBE YUKI-KUN...
...SAW IT, TOO.
.....
AH.
NO...
WHEN I THOUGHT THAT...

MAYBE I'M JUST WORRYING OVER NOTHING. BUT...
...I'M AFRAID TO ASK ABOUT IT.
BUT...
KAGURA-SAN ACTED LIKE SHE KNEW ABOUT HIS TRUE FORM.
MAYBE YUKI-KUN ALREADY KNEW ABOUT IT, TOO.
I MIGHT TOUCH ON THINGS THAT THEY DON'T WANT TO BE TOUCHED.
FOR THAT REASON...
...IN FRONT OF KAGURA-SAN AND YUKI-KUN...
...ALL I CAN DO IS ACT LIKE I DON'T KNOW.
pat

EH?
UH!
Look over here! Look over here!
Turn this way!
?
ポン ポン
pat pat pat
...NN.
LATER.
turn
HUH?

step
YOU SEEM...
...PRETTY DOWN.
DID SOME-THING...
...HAPPEN?
.....
I'M TRYING SO HARD TO FIGHT IT.
DON'T SAY THINGS LIKE THAT.
YOU'RE "FIGHTING IT"?
!
HARU... HOW'S KAGURA DOING?
HOW SHOULD I KNOW? I HARDLY EVER SEE HER.
BUT, I THINK SHE'S DOING ALL RIGHT...
Our houses are far apart.

DID SOMETHING HAPPEN TO KAGURA-NEE?
-nee: honorific for "big sister."
KAGURA, ARE YOU LEAVING?
EVERYONE'S STILL ASLEEP.
YEAH... BUT TODAY I'M KIND OF...
WILL YOU JUST TELL KYO-KUN... I'LL SEE HIM LATER? OKAY, YUN-CHAN?
KAGURA ...
NN?
YOU'RE WEIRD, YUN-CHAN.
.....
IT...IT'S NOTHING.
EEH? WHAT IS IT?
KAGURA IS... STRONG.

FOR NOW, I'LL KEEP A LID ON IT.
IF I DON'T, THE MUDDY FEELINGS WILL OVER-FLOW.
HATRED, DISGUST...
I'LL BE SWALLOWED UP BY THOSE DIRTY FEELINGS AGAIN.
I DON'T WANT THAT ANYMORE.
SOME-THING DID HAPPEN...
...BUT...
...SHE WON'T SAY.
MAYBE SOMEDAY ...
...WHEN I'M A BETTER PERSON...
BUT...
FOR NOW, I'LL KEEP A LID ON IT...A TIGHT LID.
THAT FORM, THE OTHER THINGS, ALL OF IT... EVERYTHING.

...SHE'S WORRIED ABOUT YOU, YOU KNOW?
HONDA-SAN.
WHETHER YOU EXPRESS YOUR FEELINGS OR NOT...
...IS YOUR CHOICE, YUKI.
BUT YOU REALLY SHOULDN'T LEAVE HER WORRYING LIKE THAT.
.....
YOU REALLY DIDN'T NOTICE?
I DIDN'T.
IT'S THE LEAST YOU COULD DO.
AND IT'S NOT JUST HONDA-SAN...
.....
I'M...
...WORRIED ABOUT YOU.
YOU'RE ALWAYS WORRYING SO MUCH ABOUT OTHER PEOPLE.

IT'S MY PERSONALITY, I GUESS.
I WANT YOU TO ENJOY LIFE.
STILL...
...I HATE WATCHING YOU SUFFER.
YOU'RE RIGHT...

HONDA-SAN.
Ah ha ha
pitter patter
YUKI-KUN!
SOME OF THE STUDENT COUNCIL MEMBERS WERE LOOKING FOR YOU.
SOMETHING ABOUT "DOING THINGS BY THE BOOK."
HONDA-SAN.
I...
I CAN TIE MY NECKTIE FASTER THAN I USED TO.
AND I CAN SOMEHOW BUTTON MY SHIRT BETTER.
AND MY VEGETABLES DON'T DIE AS OFTEN.
AND I THINK... I'M MORE COMFORTABLE TALKING TO PEOPLE NOW.

...THAT I TOLD KISA I WOULD BECOME.
BUT I STILL HAVE A LONG WAY TO GO.
HONDA-SAN...
I'VE WORRIED YOU.
!
MAYBE I'LL BE ABLE TO OPEN THE LID I'VE CLOSED SO TIGHTLY...
...WITHOUT BEING SWALLOWED UP.
MAYBE SOMEDAY I CAN BECOME THAT PERSON...
I KNOW THESE ARE JUST LITTLE THINGS...
...BUT BY DOING THEM...
...I THINK I'M GETTING CLOSER TO TRYING THE THINGS I COULDN'T STAND BEFORE.
EVEN IF IT'S JUST A LITTLE BIT AT A TIME...
...IT'S HELPING ME TO WORK THROUGH MY ISSUES.

...HONDA-SAN.
...THAT I'M NOT READY TO TELL YOU...
THERE'S STILL A LOT...
?!!
I'M SORRY.
EH?!
OH NO, YOU DON'T HAVE TO DO THAT! I JUST...!
I'M STILL... SO PATHETIC.
...BY LITTLE.
BUT...
...I WILL. LITTLE...
I'LL GAIN THE COURAGE...
...TO TELL YOU.
OKAY.

AND THIS SUMMER...
...I THINK I'LL SPEND A LOT OF TIME OUTSIDE.
IT SEEMS LIKE I COULD BUILD A LOT OF NEW MEMORIES...
Ah!
YOU MEAN YOU THINK YOU COULD LIKE SUMMER?!
UH-HUH. WHEN I THOUGHT ABOUT IT, I REALIZED THAT I MIGHT REALLY ENJOY IT.
FIRE-WORKS, AND FESTIVALS, AND THE OCEAN...
...WITH YOU, HONDA-SAN.
!
YOU... DON'T WANT TO?
EH?!
N-NO, OF COURSE I WANT TO...!
IF YOU DON'T COME ALONG WILL-INGLY...

...I'LL KIDNAP YOU.
YOU'D BETTER WATCH OUT.
...KIDDING!
JUST...
?!!

HONDA-SAN?!
BANG
BUCKLE
A-ARE YOU OKAY?!
I-I-I'M OKAY. I'M FINE!
I-I WAS JUST SO SURPRISED, THAT IS...UM...
I'M SORRY.
AH HA HA HA!
pfft!
...HA!
HA HA!

YUKI-KUN AND KYO-KUN...
...ARE BECOMING MORE AND MORE WONDERFUL.
EVERYTHING ABOUT THEM, INSIDE AND OUT...
Sorry, sorry.
I shouldn't laugh.
You alright?
OF COURSE YOU'RE NOT, YUKI-KUN.
"PATHETIC"?
....IS SO WONDERFUL THAT I'M AFRAID...
...MY HEART WILL SOON GIVE OUT.
WHY IS HARU COMING HOME WITH US?

I'LL MAKE SOMETHING YOU LIKE, HATSUHARU-SAN!
I WAS INVITED TO DINNER.
.....? SO WHY IS THIS GOING ON?
empty-handed.

I START GOING TO SHISHOU'S TODAY.
SAVE SOME DINNER FOR ME.
I'll eat it later.
OKAY! PLEASE DO YOUR BES--

Ky—
o—

IT'S OUR...
...LITTLE SECRET.
WHATEVER.
I was stupid for expecting a serious answer.

KUN!!
I'm so HAPPY!
YOU'RE NOT RUNNING AWAY FROM ME TODAY!
THUNK...
SHE'S GOT HIM PINNED.
KA...
KAGURA-SA...?

I DECIDED TO START GOING AGAIN, TOO.
DRAG
ALL RIGHT, KYO-KUN, LET'S GO!
WHERE ARE YOU TAKING HIM?
DRAG
DRAG
DRAG
snap!
?!!
Huh?
TO SHIHAN'S DOJO!

YOU'RE COMING ALONG NICE AND EASY, RIGHT?!
strangle
strangle
strangle
I DON'T KNOW IF THAT'S THE BEST WAY TO CONVINCE HIM.
Oh well.

SHE SEEMS TO BE IN GOOD SPIRITS.
You—how can you just...
Now we can see each other three times a week!
tee hee!

SHE'S GETTING THERE.
KAGURA IS... WELL, SHE'S KAGURA.
.....

'KAY, SEE YOU LATER! ♡
YUN-CHAN, HARU-CHAN!
TOHRU-KUN!
YES!
HAVE A SAFE TRIP!
THERE ARE TIMES...
...WE WANT TO RUN AWAY.
I'm glad; it looks like we'll be able to have a quiet dinner
Gone like the wind...

BUT WE'RE LEARNING TO COPE...
ALL OF US.
THERE ARE ONLY THREE MEN IN THIS WORLD WHO WOULD GO TO SUCH LENGTHS FOR THEIR YOUNGER BROTHERS. AND OF COURSE, NUMBER ONE AMONG THEM IS NONE OTHER THAN MYSELF!
WHEN I SUDDENLY FOUND MYSELF IN POSSESSION OF ALL THIS MAGINIFICENT CRAB, I KNEW I SIMPLY MUST SHARE IT WITH YUKI, AND SO I CAME HERE FORTHWITH!
WHAT DO I HAVE TO HIDE? EAT AS MUCH CRAB AS YOU LIKE!
HA! HA!
This crab miso is delicious!
HA!
HA!
HA!
OH MY!
WHAT COULD BE THE MATTER, YUKI? CLEARLY YOU ARE GAZING OFF INTO THE DISTANCE.
GOOD LUCK, YUKI.
Fight.
OF COURSE, OF COURSE! I UNDERSTAND!
YOUR EYES ARE SPINNING BECAUSE OF THE MATCHLESS LOVE OF YOUR OLDER BROTHER!

Chapter 36

I feel so grateful!

Harada-sama, Araki-sama, Kawai-sama, Mom, Dad, and everyone who reads this and supports me, I couldn't have done it without you!

Hatori, you're up next!

This has been Natsuki Takaya

ULTRA-SPECIAL BLAH BLAH BLAH 4

Ever since I started drawing this manga, I thought, "I want to draw a color picture of Kyo smiling!" And so, his first smile. That doesn't mean he'll always be smiling, though. This boy really is hopeless. (laugh)

*Nii-san: older brother

...IS TRYING TO CHANGE HIS RELATIONSHIP...
...WITH AYAME-SAN.
.....
?!
SO...
YUKI-KUN...
LISTEN TO THIS, GURE-SAN!!
YUKI--YES, THAT YUKI--
--CAME TO ME WITH TEARS IN HIS EYES SAYING THAT BY ALL MEANS HE WOULD LIKE TO COME VISIT ME AT MY SHOP!!
YES?

LISTEN TO THIS, TORI-SAN!
YUKI!! YES, THAT YUKI!!
STOP THAT !!!
Has there even been such a joyous day as this?! No, I dare say there has not!
Nii-sa...
OH! It's too good to be true!
CLACK
カチャ。
That said, it would be perfectly fine if you did not come, Kyonkichi.
WHAT ARE YOU DOING BARGING INTO MY ROOM AND SPOUTING OFF YOUR NONSENSE?
Get out, psycho.
Yes, yes. Of course you are welcome. I'd be honored!
You may come as early as this Sunday!
ER...
And Tohru-kun! You simply must come, too!
EH?
A prince must always have a princess by his side!

Fruits Basket 6 Part 6:

In the last volume, I talked about what kind of snacks I liked at the time, but since then I've moved from "fugashi" to "egg booro" and now it's Choco-Balls (with caramel!). What toy did it come with...? Since I was a kid, it made me wonder. I was one of those kids who thinks, "I wanna hurry and grow up!" There were a lot of reasons, and one of them was, "So I'll be able to eat as many 'cucumber shrimp sen' as I want!" In hindsight, that's a pretty petty reason to want to grow up (laugh). But now that I can buy things with money I earned myself, that dream has come true. It was a very happy revelation.

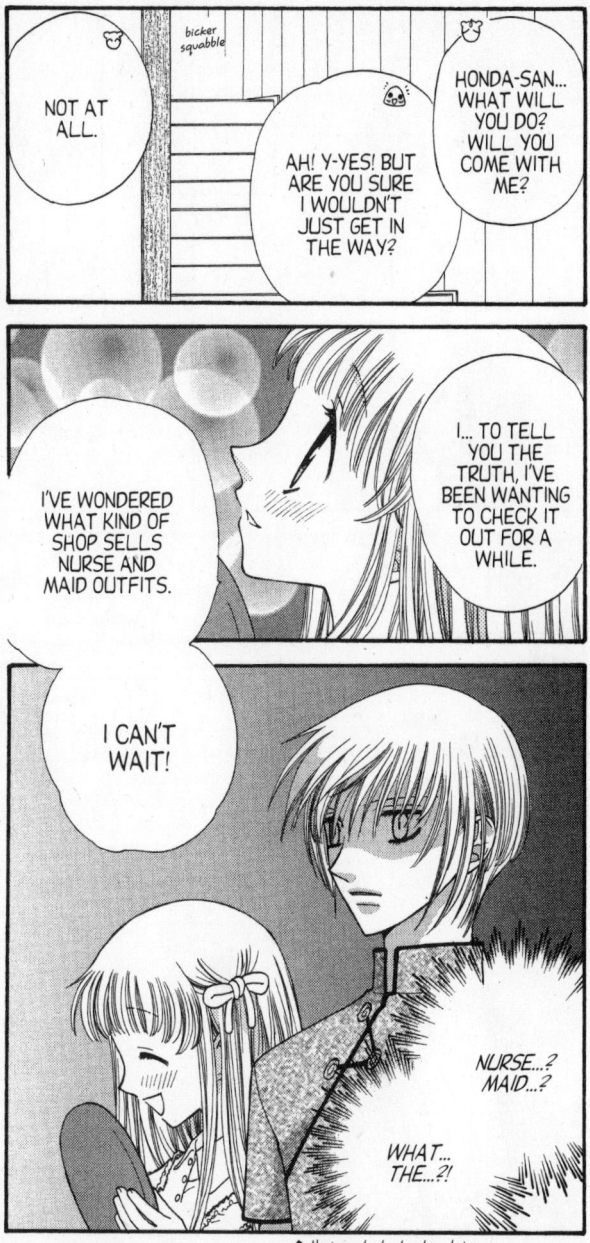

↑ He knew he had a shop, but he had no idea what it sold.

WELL...
LET'S GET THIS OVER WITH.
THAT BRINGS US TO TODAY.
End of Flashback
OKAY!
THIS COULD ALL END BADLY. VERY BADLY.
AND...
...SO...
A CRAFT...
...SHOP?
I'M SORRY, SIR, BUT...
...WE'RE CLOSED TO-
コト。
.....

* "Mine" is a woman's name. It's pronounced "Me-nay."

Yuukíííí!
SOMETHING'S COMING...
SOMETHING...
SOMETHING STRANGE!!
HA! HA! HA!
MY APOLOGIES. WE WERE HEMMING A WEDDING DRESS THAT SOMEONE HAD ORDERED.
BUT OF COURSE! BECAUSE THE ONE WHO WANTS IT IS A MAN.
SHOULD YOU BE MEASURING IT ON A MAN?

EVERYONE HAS ONE, TWO, OR THREE SECRET GARDENS THAT THEY CAN'T SHARE WITH ANYONE.
THAT DRESS...
...IS FOR A MAN?
doom doom
S...
SO... WHAT IS THIS... SHOP?
doom doom doom
slump
!!
I, AS OWNER OF THIS ESTABLISHMENT, WILL TAILOR ANY CLOTHES THAT ARE ORDERED.
NO DESIGN IS AN ENEMY TO ME.
...AND FOR THOSE WHOSE FASHION DREAMS INVOLVE DRESSING AS HANDMAIDS.
ELEMENTARY, MY DEAR BROTHER!
IT'S A SHOP FOR THOSE WHO WANT THEIR DREAMS FASHIONED INTO THE FINEST HANDMADE DRESSINGS...

UWAHH!
THESE ARE BUT A SAMPLING OF MY COMPLETED WORKS!
Out with it.
WHY ARE THEY ALL THOSE KIND OF CLOTHES?
WHAT DO YOU THINK, YUKI?
GO AHEAD. YOU MAY PRAISE ME AS WELL.
SO THIS IS WHAT HATSU-HARU-SAN WAS TALKING ABOUT!
AMAZING...! IT'S AMAZING, AYAME-SAN!
But of course!
I AM AMAZING!!
.....!
But of course!
IT MAY BE DIFFICULT FOR YOU TO UNDERSTAND NOW, YUKI, BUT THESE ARE ALL FORMS OF...
THEY'RE... POPULAR ...?
BECAUSE THEY'RE VERY POPULAR!
The maid is the most popular.

MEN'S ROMANCE!
MAIDS AND NURSES, WAITRESSES AND STEWARD-ESSES AND SECRETARIES!
SAILOR SUITS AND CAT EARS, RABBIT EARS... THERE'S TOO MANY TO LIST!
IN THESE SIMPLE FASHIONS, MEN CHASE THEIR DREAMS AND BRING THEIR ROMANTIC FANTASIES TO LIFE! THERE'S NO CRIME IN PURSUING YOUR DREAMS TO ESCAPE THE HARSH REALITY OF LIFE.
IT'S NO DIFFERENT FROM THE ROMANTIC URGE TO PEEK INTO A WOMAN'S BATH!!
THAT'S ILLEGAL!!

Mm-hmm.
HE'S EXACTLY LIKE YOU, BOSS! AT LEAST, ON THE OUTSIDE.
HA! HA! HA! HA!
creak...
YOU SEEM TO BE HAVING FUN.
I WAS WONDERING WHY YOU SUDDENLY DECIDED TO CLOSE SHOP TODAY.
YOU NEVER TOLD ME YOUR LITTLE BROTHER WAS COMING!
Ah...
PLEASED TO MEET ...
GASP
UM... WOULD THAT OUTFIT HAPPEN TO BE...
...THIS STORE'S UNIFORM?
EH? OH, NO.
PLEASED TO MEET YOU, OTOUTO-KUN!
I'M MINE KURAMAE. I WORK FOR YOUR BROTHER!
I ALSO HELP MAKE THE CLOTHES!
otouto-kun: little brother

キラーン
sparkle
THIS HAS BEEN BOTHERING ME FOR A WHILE, BUT--
YOU THERE!
EH ?!
Y-YES! PLEASED TO MEET YOU! I'M TOHRU HONDA...
TOHRU-CHAN!
ARE YOU INTERESTED IN CLOTHES LIKE THESE?!
Isn't it cute!?!
I'M WEARING THIS BECAUSE I LIKE IT!
It's adorable!
WHEN MINE SEES A CUTE GIRL, SHE HAS A TENDENCY OF WANTING TO MAKE HER CHANGE CLOTHES.
MUA HA HA HA!
Shall we try something on? ♡
!!?
EH?
WOULD YOU LIKE TO WEAR THEM? WOULDN'T YOU? YOU WOULD, RIGHT!?!
Mm.
IT SEEMS IT HAS BEGUN.
?

I SAID HOLD ON!!
OTOUTO-KUN!! WHAT WOULD YOU LIKE TOHRU-CHAN TO WEAR?! DEFINITELY SOMETHING PROPER...
PL–
PLEASE, HOLD ON! KURAMAE-SAN!

THAT ONE, BOSS?!
WHAT IS "THAT ONE"!?!
THAT ONE IS THE MOST CHARMING, ISN'T IT?!
MINE. I THINK IN THIS CASE, THAT ONE WOULD BE THE BEST.

THERE'S NO HELPING HER NOW, YUKI. SHE'S IN MINE'S CLUTCHES!
NOT TO WORRY, THOUGH. I'M SURE MINE WILL GO EASY ON HER.
It's locked.

QUICKLY, TOHRU-CHAN!!
LET US BEGIN YOUR TRANSFORMATION INTO THAT!!
SLAM
!!
click☆

THEY PROBABLY DON'T NEED OUR HELP, SO AS LONG AS YOU'RE HERE...
...WILL YOU COOPERATE?
YES!
.....
NOW THE TWO BROTHERS CAN SPEND SOME QUALITY TIME ALONE.
!!
I JUST HOPE THEY CAN TALK WITHOUT FIGHTING.
OH!
A FIGHT WOULD BE GOOD!!
IT'S PROOF THAT THEY'RE ACTUALLY ACKNOWLEDGING EACH OTHER!
BECAUSE WHAT BOSS IS MOST AFRAID OF...
.....
...IS "NOTHING-NESS."

BUT I WOULD LIKE FOR THEM TO AVOID ACTUALLY SPILLING BLOOD.
IT WOULD BE A PROBLEM IF BLOOD GOT ON THE MERCHANDISE.
AH HA HA...
.....
SHE'S RIGHT. IF PEOPLE REALLY ACKNOWLEDGE EACH OTHER...
...SOMETIMES THEY'LL END UP FIGHTING.
NOW!
PUTTING THAT ASIDE...
Let's change your clothes, shall we...? ♡
HA
HA
MUA
EH?!
YOU'RE REALLY GOING TO CHANGE MY CLOTHES?!
Of course!!

THAT'S NOT AT ALL WHY.
I REALLY CANNOT HELP BUT THINK THAT IT IS BECAUSE YOU HAVE BEEN INFLUENCED BY ME, YOUR OLDER BROTHER!
I UNDERSTAND THAT YOU'VE DECIDED TO BECOME STUDENT BODY PRESIDENT, YUKI?
I heard from Gure-san.
...
JUST LIKE HOW, TO ME, THIS SHOP IS BAFFLING.
OUR WAYS OF THINKING ARE TOO DIFFERENT.
WHATEVER DO YOU MEAN?
TRULY, THAT IS A MOST BAFFLING MOTIVATION.
clink
.....
TO SOMEONE LIKE YOU, I GUESS IT WOULD BE.
YOUNGER BROTHERS ALWAYS ASPIRE TO BE LIKE THEIR OLDER BROTHERS...
I SAID THAT'S NOT IT!!
I DID IT BECAUSE I DIDN'T WANT TO!!

MAYBE, IN THE END... WE JUST DON'T SEE EYE TO EYE
MM!!
THERE IS SOME TRUTH IN THAT!
DON'T BE SO POSITIVE ABOUT IT!!
BUT YOU MUSTN'T LOSE HEART! A JOURNEY OF A THOUSAND MILES BEGINS WITH A SINGLE STEP! DON'T SPARE ANY EFFORT!
YOU PUT FORTH A LITTLE EFFORT TOO, NII-SAN!!
FORGIVE ME! I MAY NOT LOOK IT, BUT I REALLY AM TRYING.
……!
fwump
とさっ
WHAT AM I SUPPOSED TO DO...?
YOU...
FORGIVE ME.

I COULDN'T HELP IT.
I'M JUST OVERJOYED THAT YOU CAME.
SEE, YOU WERE ALWAYS SO ANGRY WITH ME...
...AND, AFTER HOW I TREATED YOU...
...I DESERVED IT.
IT'S NOT AS IF I'VE FORGOTTEN.
I WAS CRUEL...
...INSENSITIVE TO YOUR PAIN.
... TREMBLING HANDS.
...YOU REACHED OUT TO ME...
...WITH THOSE...
THE FIRST AND ONLY TIME YOU CAME TO ME FOR HELP...

AND I JUST BRUSHED YOU OFF.
TO ME, THERE WAS NEVER ANY LOVE OR HATE FOR YUKI—HE WAS 'NOTHING' TO ME.
BUT WHEN I GOT OLDER AND REALIZED THAT YUKI MIGHT NEVER BE INTERESTED IN HAVING A RELATIONSHIP WITH ME...
...FOR THE FIRST TIME, I FELT TERRIFYINGLY LONELY.
IT'S NOT AS IF I'VE FORGOTTEN.
I FINALLY KNEW HOW IT FELT...
...TO BE TREATED AS NOTHING.

WHEN I REALIZED THIS, I WAS AFRAID IT WAS TOO LATE.
BUT TODAY, YUKI...
...LOOKED AT ME.
HE LISTENED TO WHAT I SAID, AND GOT ANGRY.
EVEN NOW, YOU'RE SITTING THERE...
...TO UNDERSTAND ME.
...AND TRYING...
.....
EVEN IF WE DON'T SEE EYE TO EYE...
...EVEN IF WE CLASH WITH EACH OTHER, WHAT'S WRONG WITH THAT?

I'M SURE...
...I HAVE QUALITIES YOU DON'T, AND YOU HAVE QUALITIES I DON'T.
WE WERE BORN THAT WAY.
I THINK THAT THE WEAKNESS...
...AND THE KINDNESS...
...THAT YOU HAVE...
...ARE VERY...
...PRECIOUS.

AND I'M SURE MY UNIQUE CHARISMA, THAT HAS SUCH AN AIR OF NOBILITY...
...IS VERY PRECIOUS TO YOU, YUKI!
Of course I understand!
LIKE I WAS SAYING ...
THIS MAN IS JUST SO...
OH!
YOU'VE FINISHED CHANGING HER CLOTHES?
NOW, COME OUT FORTHWITH!
YOU HEARD HIM, TOHRU-CHAN!
COME OUT FORTHWITH!
AH!
OH YEAH...
creak
HEY, BOSS! AM I INTERRUPTING ANYTHING?

WH...
WHAT DO YOU THINK?
C'EST MAGNIFIQUE!!
HA! HA! HA! HA!
TOHRU-KUN REALLY DOES BECOME THE SWEET, PURE IMAGE OF A GIRL HOLDING A WHITE LACE PARASOL, LEADING A WHITE DOG.
MM-HM. DRINKING ENGLISH TEA, READING POETRY BY A WHITE WINDOW WITH WHITE LACE CURTAINS! ♡
She has no idea how to react
HUH?!
UH...
WHAT IS THIS? AND WHEN A GIRL IS DRESSED UP SO CHARMINGLY, TOO. HOW DISAPPOINTING.
IN THAT CASE...
COME ON,YUKI! GIVE HER SOME PRAISE!

DON'T!!
I WILL GIVE HER A KISS TO EXPRESS MY DELIGHT!
O-ohhh!
I'M HONORED!
I PRAISE YOUR FINE CRAFTSMANSHIP.
TOHRU-KUN HAS A WONDERFUL AIR OF CUTENESS.
Silly!
HE HIT ME!
ANY GENTLEMAN WOULD HAVE HIT YOU, I'M SURE.
HA! HA! HA! HA! HA!
WELL?
NN? I WONDER.
I DON'T REALLY KNOW.
WERE YOU ABLE TO WORK THINGS OUT A LITTLE WITH YOUR BROTHER?

IN THE END, MAYBE I WAS THE ONLY ONE ...
...WHO FELT HAPPY ABOUT IT, ONCE AGAIN.
HONDA-SAN...
I WAS ABLE TO UNDER-STAND ONE THING ABOUT MY BROTHER.
EH?
...ALMOST EVERYTHING MY BROTHER SAYS AND DOES IS COMPLETE NONSENSE.
THERE'S NO AVOIDING IT...

HE'S LIKE AN UNSTOPPABLE FORCE OF NATURE. IT'S USELESS TO FIGHT IT. WHEN I TRY, I JUST GET EXHAUSTED.
I...I SEE.
SOMEHOW... SAYING THAT MAKES ME SAD...
BUT...
...IN SPITE OF THAT...
...I'M GLAD I CAME.
.....
...IF I HADN'T, I WOULDN'T HAVE GOT TO SEE YOU LOOKING SO CUTE.
BESIDES ...

AH!
NOT AT ALL... UM...!
NO, THAT...!
.....!
DON'T HIDE IT...

ROMANCE.
YOU SEE?
HUH ...?
THE FEELING THAT HAS NOW SPROUTED IN YOUR HEART IS WHAT IS A CALLED A MAN'S ROMANTIC FANTASY!
A MAN IS A BEING WHOSE HEART IS SWAYED BY A SINGLE COSTUME, AFTER ALL.
WHA ...?
THIS IS GOOD! I UNDERSTAND. OF COURSE I UNDERSTAND! THIS WONDERFUL DAY SHALL BE KNOWN AS--
The Day of Yuki's Romantic Fantasy!
THEY'RE FIGHTING AFTER ALL.
CUT. IT. OUT !!

To be continued in Volume 7...

Next time in...

New kid on the block...

Tohru and company have been having a lot more fun ever since Kisa came to visit. Now it's time for Tohru to meet another member of the Zodiac--the skillfully sarcastic grade-school student, Hiro! One way or another, this tyke will have to deal with his resentment of Tohru and his affection for Kisa!

Fruits Basket Volume 7
Available Feburary 2005

Year of the Rabbit: Splitting Hares

Rabbit

Years': 1939, 1951, 1963, 1975, 1987, 1999, 2011, 2023, 2035
Positive Qualities: sympathetic, affectionate, humble, creative, optimistic
Negative Qualities: too sentimental, avoids conflict
Suitable Jobs: Diplomat, Lawyer, College Professor, Actor
Compatible With: Sheep, Boar and Rat
Must Avoid: Rooster, Tiger and Horse
Ruling Hours: 5 AM to 7 AM
Season: Spring
Ruling Month: March
Sign Direction: East
Fixed Element: Wood
Corresponding Western Sign: Pisces

Men born in the year of the Rabbit tend to be courteous and refined, and carry themselves like true gentlemen. They are resourceful, and are often sought out for their strong advice, but they tend to think quite unrealistically and have a hard time dealing with misfortune.

Female Rabbits tend to be very serious people, but they love company. Among friends, they are very considerate and caring; however, when it comes to their taste in men, women rabbits tend to be more insecure, dating guys who shower them with gifts.

Celebrity Rabbits:
Tori Amos
Aaron Carter
Phoebe Cates
Whitney Houston
Angelina Jolie
Mark McGwire
Mike Myers
Bugs Bunny

The year of the Rabbit--a calm year where everyone is more leisurely than normal and where days go by at seemingly carefree pace. For anyone born in this year, luck will surely follow. However, like Momiji Sohma, Rabbits often have are seen to have a frail outward appearance because they are so gentle-natured, but deep within they are strong-minded and very idealistic.

Rabbits make great companions, and their marriages are usually free of strife. Rabbits keep a mental record of both a person's good points and their mistakes, but they tend to be very forgiving as long as the mistakes do not have dire consequences. But even as Rabbits are good at offering support and advice, they find it difficult to accept advice or criticism from others. Their desire to avoid conflict can make them come off as overly sentimental or even superficial, making deep emotional connections difficult. But when it happens, the relationships they form are very strong.

* Note: If you were born in January or early February, then chances are you are probably the animal of the preceding year. The only way to know for certain is to know on which day Chinese New Year's was held. Example: 1987 actually began on January 29, so anyone born between January 1 and January 28 is actually a Tiger.

Fans Basket

Kylie B.
Age 12
Danbury, CT

Princess Tohru

Tohru Honda is like a princess
To Yuki and Kyo she is truly a bless

Shigure's house was a huge mess
But now it's clean thanks to the princess

Tohru has a terrible past
But like Momiji, she makes memories last

Kyo sometimes calls her stupid
But Arisa says he was hit by Cupid

Akito called her an ugly girl
His head must be in a whirl

For Tohru is pretty inside and out
For Momiji and me that fact is no doubt

Tohru has made family and friends
The Sohmas will stick with her to the end

What a lovely poem. And a matching picture, too! Thanks so much!

LaDonna L.
AZ

This picture is a lot of fun. Love the T-shirts! But I have a hard time imagining Yuki wearing Tie-Dye...

KT SHY
Age 20
Ontario, Canada

Shigure has been Disneyfied! He's adorable! Thanks so much KT. (I loved your Peach Girl fan art, too!)

LaDonna L.
AZ

Tohru Honda had a farm, E-I-E-I-O!
Thank goodness there isn't a year of the Elephant–otherwise the Sohma household would be in trouble!

Male K.
Age 19
Austin, TX

Yuki and Kyo linking arms?! I love it!
Your style is so unique. Thank you so much.

Christy S.
Age 27
Gainesville, FL

Momiji! Our cover boy.
Look at all those pins–the entire jumishi!
And an onigiri in his hand. Great idea!

"Sora"
Age 14
Sierra Vista, AZ

Tohru in a Yukata. And she's wearing Yuki's ribbon! I wonder if we'll get to see the onsen again?

Melyssa M.
Age 16
Las Vegas, NV

The many faces of Tohru Honda.
Your drawings are so expressive. Very cute! I like them all.

Erin B.
Age 12
Oakdale, NY

The two brothers. They're finally getting closer!
Wasn't Ayame's shop great?

Do you want to share your love for *Fruits Basket* with fans around the world? "Fans Basket" is taking submissions of fan art, poetry, cosplay photos, or any other Furuba fun you'd like to share!

How to submit:

1) Send your work via regular mail (NOT e-mail) to:

"Fans Basket"
c/o TOKYOPOP
5900 Wilshire Blvd.
Suite 2000
Los Angeles, CA 90036

2) All work should be in black-and-white and no larger than 8.5" x 11". (And try not to fold it too many times!)

3) Anything you send will not be returned. If you want to keep your original, it's fine to send us a copy.

4) Please include your full name, age, city and state for us to print with your work. If you'd rather us use a pen name, please include that, too.

5) IMPORTANT: If you're under the age of 18, you must have your parent's permission in order for us to print your work. Any submissions without a signed note of parental consent cannot be used.

6) For full details, please check out our website: http://www.tokyopop.com/aboutus/fanart.php

Disclaimer: Anything you send to us becomes the exclusive property of TOKYOPOP Inc. and, as we said before, will not be returned to you. We will have the right to print, reproduce, distribute, or modify the artwork for use in future volumes of Fruits Basket or on the web royalty-free.

Courtney R.
Age 13
New Smyrna Beach, FL

Yuki Sohma by way of Kaori Yuki!
What a great concept! And the chain on Kyo's collar... Daisuki desu!

"Kuro-neko"
Age 14
Mount Washington KY

Shigure in cargo pants! Now that's a look we'll probably never see in the pages of Furuba! And a braid! Very cool.

Malie-chan
Age 16
Cimarron, KA

Not just a picture, but a fan fiction story, too! Thanks for a wonderful read, Malie-chan. I'm sorry we didn't have room to print your story, too.

Erin S.
Age 13
Maple Grove, M

Look at those snuggle buddies. Such a peaceful picture. I wonder what they're dreaming of?

Theodore W.
Age 16
Brooklyn, NY

Haru and his accessories. "What exactly is the pendant on the left," Theodore asks—"a blade or a person?" Good question! Theodore also asks how Haru and Momiji can both be the same age if they're different Zodiac years. Well, the truth is that the cursed Sohma weren't necessarily born on the same year as their Zodiac sign. Just like Momiji and Haru are the same age, the Mabudachi Trio are also the same age. I guess those lucky 13 members are the only people in the world immune to the character dictating qualities of their birthday year! Oh, and a very nice Hatsuharu pic, Theodore. Thanks for representing the Y chromosome in this very girly month. Boy power!

Fruits Basket
FRUITS-BASKET.COM
GET CURSED!
"YOU'LL LAUGH. YOU'LL CRY. YOU'LL SAY. 'DID THAT BOY JUST TURN INTO A CAT?'"
-PLAY MAGAZINE
Tohru Honda is a cheerful 16 year old girl, who just happens to live with the Sohma family. And by the way... they are cursed.
What happens when Tohru discovers the family secret? You've got to watch to find out!
BOX SET AVAILABLE NOVEMBER 9TH
VOLUMES 1-4 AVAILABLE NOW
Imagine hugging a boy, and he turns into a cat. Wouldn't that be PURRfect?!
VIEW THE EXTENDED TRAILER ONLINE!
www.fruits-basket.com
FUNimation Productions, Ltd.
Stone.com
SUNCOAST
amazon.com
BEST BUY
fye
Fruits Basket - © 2004 Natsuki Takaya/HAKUSENSHA - TV TOKYO - NAS - Fruba Project. Licensed by FUNimation® Productions, Ltd. All Rights Reserved.

TOKYOPOP®

SHOP TOKYOPOP

WE NEVER CLOSE!

.:HOME .:ACCOUNT .:RELEASE CALENDAR .:BROWSE .:SHOPPING CART .:CHECK OUT

.:LOG IN

Welcome!
Sign in

.:SHOPPING CART

Rave Master Volume 8(1)
Princess Ai Volume 1(1)
Gundam Technical Manuals 08th MS Team(1)
Sgt. Frog Volume 1(1)

Subtotal: $33.96

View Cart Checkout

.:BEST SELLERS

Fruits Basket
A.I. Love You
Sgt. Frog
Saiyuki

.:BLOWOUT BIN

Gundam T. Man.: GWing
Gundam T. Man.: 08th
Gundam T. Man.: Stardust
Gundam T. Man.: Char's

.:SHOP BY GENRE

ACTION
HORROR
DRAMA
ROMANCE
COMEDY
FANTASY
MYSTERY
SCI-FI

.:SHOP BY CATEGORY

MANGA
ART BOOKS

NEW IN JULY!

Welcome to the off
TOKYOPOP SHOP
Come and find all
favorite MANGA t
Enjoy your shopp
here at the officia
TOKYOPOP SHO

NEW IN APRIL!

1. DN Angel V.1
2. King of Hell
3. Suki V.2
4. Samurai De
V.6
5. Mink V.1

View full list

BEST SELLERS

ON SALE 50% OFF

TECHNICAL MANUAL

COMING

www.TOKYOPOP.com/shop

Manga · Cine-Manga® · Novels

- Look for special offers!
- Pre-order upcoming releases!
- Complete your collections!

TOKYOPOP
WHEN AMANDA *FINALLY* GETS THE PET THAT SHE'S ALWAYS WANTED, THERE'S JUST ONE PROBLEM: SHE AND PEACH DON'T EXACTLY SEE EYE TO EYE! *PEACH FUZZ* SHOWS US THAT ALL FRIENDS CAN BE HARD TO UNDERSTAND... ESPECIALLY FURRY ONES WITH SHARP TEETH!
Peach Fuzz
SCRATCH-N-SNIFF!
LINDSEY GIBBS • JARED HODGES
Peach Fuzz™
FROM THE GRAND PRIZE WINNERS OF TOKYOPOP'S SECOND *RISING STARS OF MANGA* COMPETITION.

TOKYOPOP®
THE EPIC STORY OF A FERRET WHO DEFIED HER CAGE.
A
ALL AGES
www.TOKYOPOP.com
©2004 JARED HODGES & LINDSAY CIBOS

ALSO AVAILABLE FROM TOKYOPOP®

PLANETES
PRESIDENT DAD
PRIEST
PRINCESS AI
PSYCHIC ACADEMY
QUEEN'S KNIGHT, THE
RAGNAROK
RAVE MASTER
REALITY CHECK
REBIRTH
REBOUND
REMOTE
RISING STARS OF MANGA
SABER MARIONETTE J
SAILOR MOON
SAINT TAIL
SAIYUKI
SAMURAI DEEPER KYO
SAMURAI GIRL REAL BOUT HIGH SCHOOL
SCRYED
SEIKAI TRILOGY, THE
SGT. FROG
SHAOLIN SISTERS
SHIRAHIME-SYO: SNOW GODDESS TALES
SHUTTERBOX
SKULL MAN, THE
SNOW DROP
SORCERER HUNTERS
STONE
SUIKODEN III
SUKI
TAROT CAFÉ, THE
THREADS OF TIME
TOKYO BABYLON
TOKYO MEW MEW
TOKYO TRIBES
TRAMPS LIKE US
UNDER THE GLASS MOON
VAMPIRE GAME
VISION OF ESCAFLOWNE, THE
WARCRAFT
WARRIORS OF TAO
WILD ACT
WISH
WORLD OF HARTZ
X-DAY
ZODIAC P.I.

NOVELS

CLAMP SCHOOL PARANORMAL INVESTIGATORS
SAILOR MOON

ART BOOKS

ART OF CARDCAPTOR SAKURA
ART OF MAGIC KNIGHT RAYEARTH, THE
PEACH: MIWA UEDA ILLUSTRATIONS
CLAMP NORTHSIDE
CLAMP SOUTHSIDE

ANIME GUIDES

COWBOY BEBOP
GUNDAM TECHNICAL MANUALS
SAILOR MOON SCOUT GUIDES

TOKYOPOP KIDS

STRAY SHEEP

CINE-MANGA™

ALADDIN
CARDCAPTORS
DUEL MASTERS
FAIRLY ODDPARENTS, THE
FAMILY GUY
FINDING NEMO
G.I. JOE SPY TROOPS
GREATEST STARS OF THE NBA: SHAQUILLE O'NEAL
GREATEST STARS OF THE NBA: TIM DUNCAN
JACKIE CHAN ADVENTURES
JIMMY NEUTRON: BOY GENIUS, THE ADVENTURES OF
KIM POSSIBLE
LILO & STITCH: THE SERIES
LIZZIE MCGUIRE
LIZZIE MCGUIRE MOVIE, THE
MALCOLM IN THE MIDDLE
POWER RANGERS: DINO THUNDER
POWER RANGERS: NINJA STORM
PRINCESS DIARIES 2
RAVE MASTER
SHREK 2
SIMPLE LIFE, THE
SPONGEBOB SQUAREPANTS
SPY KIDS 2
SPY KIDS 3-D: GAME OVER
TEENAGE MUTANT NINJA TURTLES
THAT'S SO RAVEN
TOTALLY SPIES
TRANSFORMERS: ARMADA
TRANSFORMERS: ENERGON

You want it? We got it!
A full range of TOKYOPOP products are available now at:
www.TOKYOPOP.com/shop

08.20.04T

Fruits Basket Vol. 6

Created by Natsuki Takaya

Translation - Alethea Nibley and Athena Nibley
Additional Translation - Alexis Kirsch
Contributing Writer - Adam Arnold
Copy Editor - Lillian Diaz-Przybyl
Retouch and Lettering - Deron Bennett
Production Artists - Yoohae Yang, James Dashiell
Cover Design - Aaron Suhr

Editor - Jake Forbes
Digital Imaging Manager - Chris Buford
Pre-Press Manager - Antonio DePietro
Production Managers - Jennifer Miller and Mutsumi Miyazaki
Art Director - Matt Alford
Managing Editor - Jill Freshney
VP of Production - Ron Klamert
President and C.O.O. - John Parker
Publisher and C.E.O. - Stuart Levy

A TOKYOPOP® Manga

TOKYOPOP Inc.
5900 Wilshire Blvd. Suite 2000
Los Angeles, CA 90036

E-mail: info@TOKYOPOP.com
Come visit us online at www.TOKYOPOP.com

FRUITS BASKET Vol. 6 by Natsuki Takaya
© 2000 Natsuki Takaya. All rights reserved.
First published in Japan in 2000 by HAKUSENSHA, INC., Tokyo English language translation rights in the United States of America and Canada arranged with HAKUSENSHA, INC., Tokyo through Tuttle-Mori Agency Inc., Tokyo
English text copyright © 2004 TOKYOPOP Inc.

All rights reserved. No portion of this book may be reproduced or transmitted in any form or by any means without written permission from the copyright holders. This manga is a work of fiction. Any resemblance to actual events or locales or persons, living or dead, is entirely coincidental.

ISBN: 1-59182-608-X

First TOKYOPOP printing: December 2004

10 9

Printed in the USA

Fruits Basket™

Volume 6

Natsuki Takaya